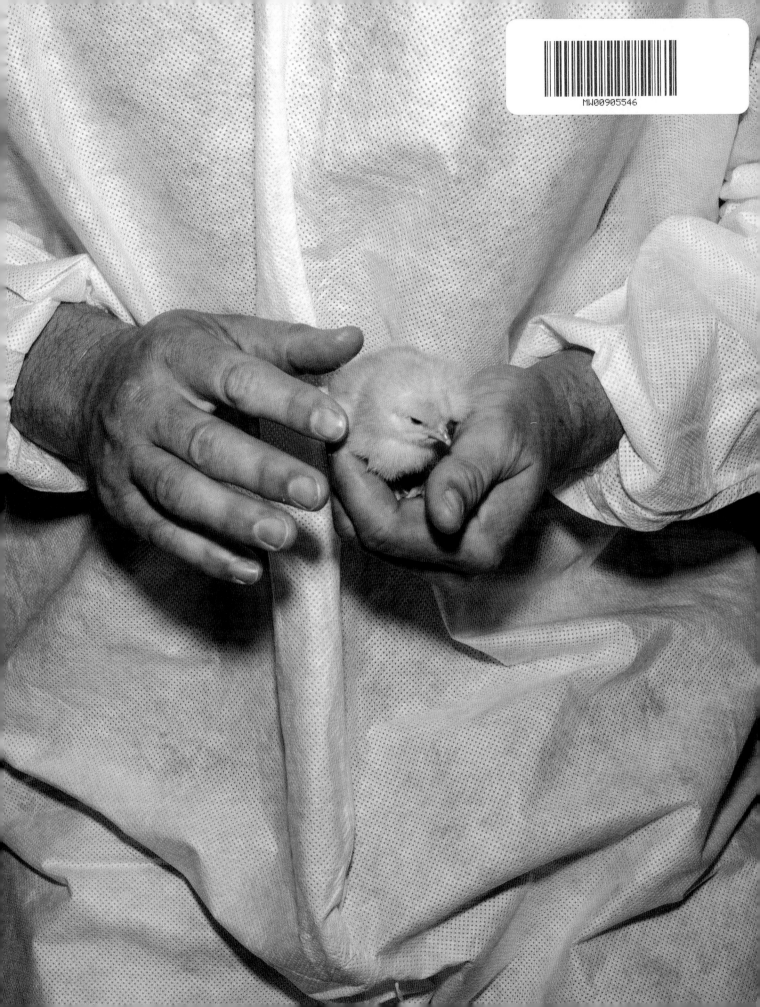

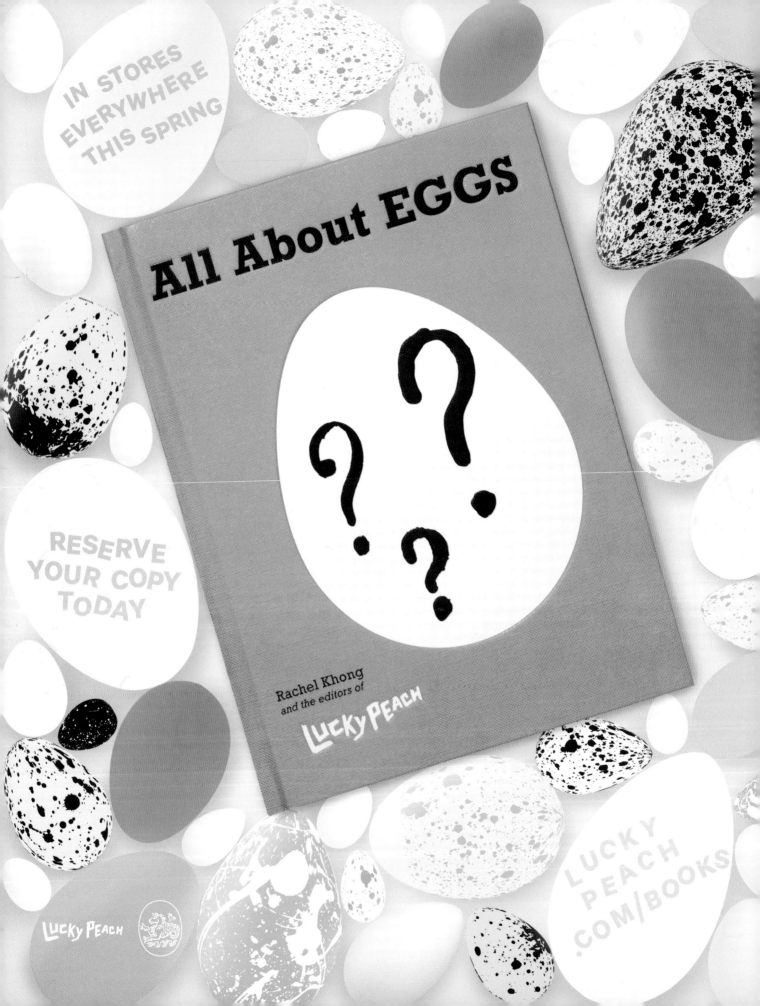

IN STORES EVERYWHERE THIS SPRING

All About EGGS

RESERVE YOUR COPY TODAY

Rachel Khong
and the editors of
LUCKY PEACH

LUCKY PEACH

LUCKY PEACH .COM/BOOKS

Lucky Peach

Farm Raised / Enhanced Chicken Product / NSFW

USLP **D** GRADE

EDITORIAL

Peter Meehan
EDITORIAL DIRECTOR

Joanna Sciarrino
MANAGING EDITOR

Aralyn Beaumont
RESEARCH EDITOR

Chris Cohen
ASSOCIATE EDITOR

Ben Mims
TEST KITCHEN DIRECTOR

Ryan Healey
WEB EDITOR

Emily Johnson
EDITORIAL ASSISTANT

Kristina Bornholtz
SOCIAL MEDIA EDITOR

Rob Engvall
ART DIRECTOR

Gabriele Stabile
ITALIAN PHOTOGRAPHER

Stephen Lurvey
JUNIOR DESIGNER

Lucky Peach (USPS 12438) (ISSN 2325-9140) is published quarterly in Spring, Summer, Fall, and Winter by Lucky Peach LLC, 128 Lafayette St., Suite 302, New York, NY 10013. Periodicals postage paid at New York, NY and additional mailing offices. POSTMASTER: Send address changes to Lucky Peach, PO Box 433324 Palm Coast, FL 32143-9559.

CanadaPost customer number 42740020.

Printed by RR Donnelley in Liberty, MO

BUSINESS

Brette Warshaw
CHIEF OPERATING OFFICER

Peter Romero
ACCOUNT EXECUTIVE

Kate Neuhaus
MARKETING MANAGER

Rachele Morino
CIRCULATION SPECIALIST

Michelle Curb
BUSINESS DEVELOPMENT

Chris Ying
EDITOR AT LARGE

CONTRIBUTING EDITORS
David Chang, Rachel Khong, Jim Meehan, Mark Ibold (SE Penn. Correspondent)

SPECIAL THANKS TO
Sascha Bos, Charlotte Goddu, Ryan Harrington, Sofia Martins, C.B. Owens, Lindsay Richardson, Kari Sonde

HELPING HANDS
Tina Battock, Hallie Delaney, Stephanie Fray, Elisandro Gonzalez-Molina, Kaj Hackinen, Misty Kalkofen, Stephen Kent, Jacob Lustig, Pablo Moix, David Muñoz, Debra Newman, Nicolas Palazzi, Éva Pelczer, William Scanlan, Tom Super

Letters, submissions, nuggets, etc. will find us at the below address

128 LAFAYETTE STREET, SUITE 302 NEW YORK, NY 10013

ADVERTISING INQUIRIES: ADS@LKY.PH
PRESS INQUIRIES: PRESS@LKY.PH
CUSTOMER SERVICE: 877-292-1504
OR 386-246-0565 (OUTSIDE THE U.S.)

READ MORE AND SUBSCRIBE AT

LUCKYPEACH.COM

ALWAYS UPDATED AND UP-TO-DATE
MADE OUT OF PIXELS INSTEAD OF PAPER

FRONT AND BACK
COVER PHOTOS BY
Gabriele Stabile

COVER PHOTOS
RETOUCHING BY
Zach Vitale

OPENING PAGE
PHOTO BY
Molly Matalon

In This Issue

Chicken: maybe you've always been curious but never experienced it. Maybe it's on your bucket list to try in 2017. Or maybe, if you're like us and large swaths of humanity in the last century, you've eaten a lot of chicken before and will eat a lot of chicken this year.

Chicken's vanilla ubiquity made it a worthy subject, but also presented a challenge: how to cover a meat that is so many things to so many people? In this, the twenty-second issue of *Lucky Peach*, we tried to open our eyes and see chicken for

what it is and what it can be. We learned how chickens are related to dinosaurs, and that washing chicken *won't* kill you and your loved ones. We found that there are chickens in Vietnam with ankles as big as your wrists, and that people love to eat them for that. There is, for your repulsion/ edification, a set of statistics on chicken production that includes a rendering of a six-hundred-pound baby.

There are a ton of recipes in this issue, because unlike, say, pho—a dish we mostly

encounter as diners—chicken is a foodstuff that's often on our stoves. Chinese-food authority Fuchsia Dunlop keeps it extra real, showing us a classic way to cook everything but the wattles and the feathers. Mary-Frances Heck, who has helped put together the recipes for all the Lucky Peach cookbooks, gives a weeknight-friendly rundown of ways to approach the bird piece by piece.

Of course, we couldn't get to everything. *Bloomberg Businessweek* beat us to the story of a Chinese chicken company deploying humanoid "nanny robots" to identify sick birds from its massive, warehoused flocks. My main takeaway was not about the prisoner-like lives of these birds in places where "bird flu is rampant"—I assume that most meat animals have it pretty shitty—but that some of the sick birds end up "next door, feeding pools of crocodiles being raised for their skin." YIKES!

And while we are silent on the topic of chicken-shit bingo, a gay and galline way to pass the drinking hours down in Austin, Texas, we do have comics peppered throughout the issue, with perhaps my most cherished chicken revelation coming from the one on the last page. But there's a lotta road to cross between here and there, so let's dive in.   **pfm 2017**

THE WORLD'S OLDEST CHICKEN LIVED TO BE SIXTEEN YEARS OLD

Chicken Comics
The bird in seven strips scattered throughout the issue

MALE CHICKENS ARE CALLED ROOSTERS

ROOSTERS UNDER ONE YEAR OLD ARE CALLED COCKERELS

This Issue's Menu

CASTRATED ROOSTERS ARE
CALLED CAPONS

A GROUP OF CHICKS
IS CALLED A CLUTCH OR
CHATTERING

ROOSTERS OVER ONE YEAR
OLD ARE CALLED COCKS

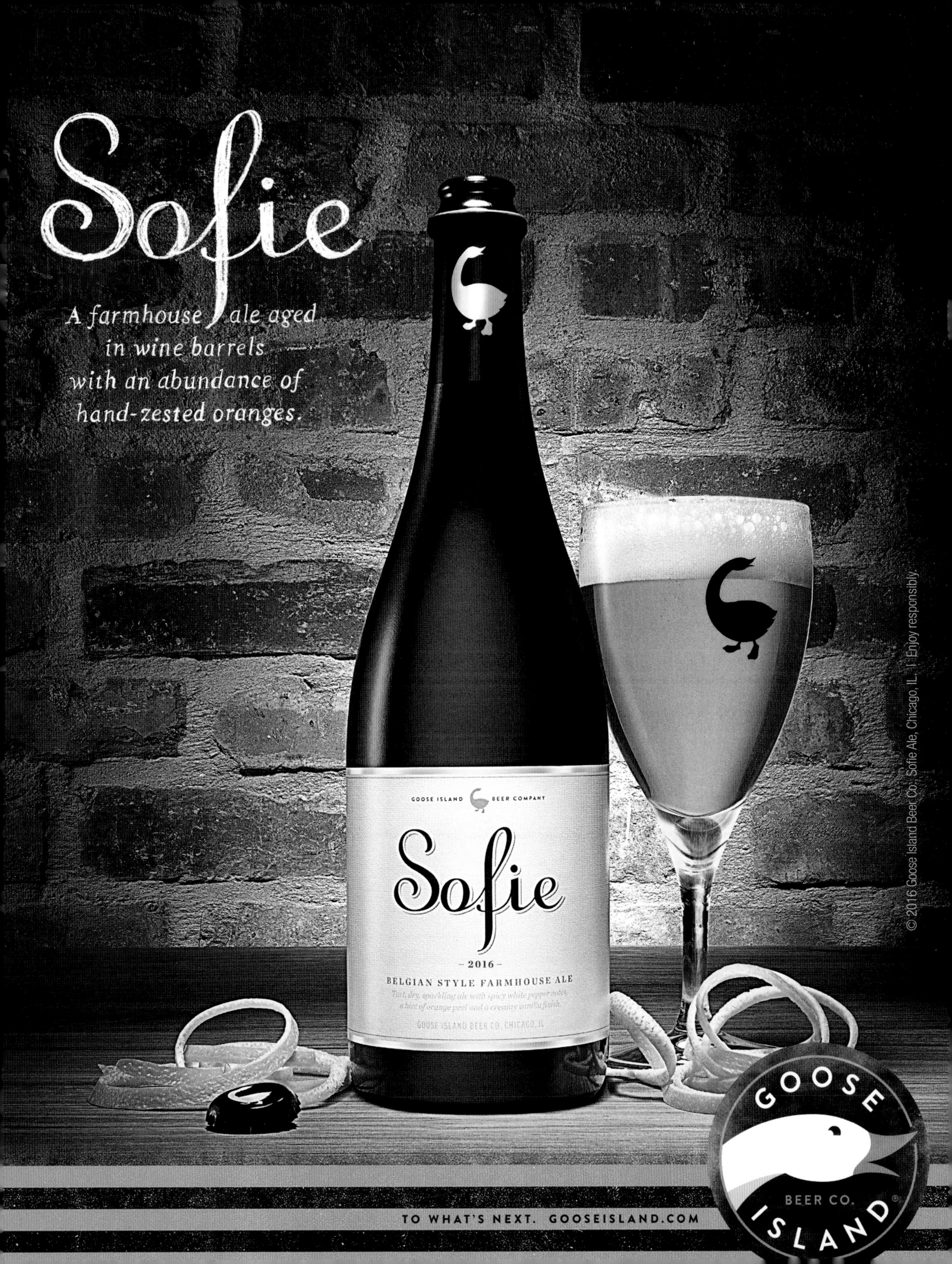

Sofie
A farmhouse ale aged in wine barrels with an abundance of hand-zested oranges.
GOOSE ISLAND BEER COMPANY
Sofie
– 2016 –
BELGIAN STYLE FARMHOUSE ALE
Tart, dry, sparkling ale with spicy white pepper notes, a hint of orange peel and a creamy vanilla finish.
GOOSE ISLAND BEER CO. CHICAGO, IL
© 2016 Goose Island Beer Co., Sofie Ale, Chicago, IL. | Enjoy responsibly.
TO WHAT'S NEXT. GOOSEISLAND.COM
GOOSE ISLAND BEER CO.®

The Lucky Peach Atlas

D'Chez Eux

Laura Goodman

Paris is the kind of city that has celebrity butchers. Every week, its most famous—Hugo Desnoyer—sets aside thirty Coucou de Rennes chickens for D'Chex Eux. The restaurant, catty-corner from Napoleon's tomb in the seventh arrondissement, has changed little since it opened in 1952. It feels a bit like the dining car of an old railway carriage, with narrow, polished wooden floors, burgundy banquettes, and checkered tablecloths. The clientele is a mix of old people who pop in once a week for their frog-leg fix, business folk from abroad who've been reserving lunches for years, and outsiders like me who come to dip their toes in the essential Frenchness of it all.

The chickens, a fussy Breton breed that takes 130 days to reach maturity and chafe in close-quarters confinement, had almost vanished by the time of their rediscovery about thirty years ago. Since then, they have become sought-after, the kind of thing you need a celebrity butcher to wrangle for you.

The roast Coucou at D'Chex Eux comes in a copper pan with creamy morel sauce, serves two, takes forty-five minutes to prepare, and costs ninety-eight euros. "It's not trivial to pay ninety-eight euros for a chicken at a restaurant," says Dominique Palvadeau, the manager, "but once you've tasted la Coucou de Rennes, you know it's worth it."

D'Chez Eux
2 Avenue de Lowendal
Paris, France

COMBS ARE THE FLESHY PROTRUSIONS ON TOP OF A CHICKEN'S HEAD AND WATTLES ARE THE TWO FLAPS OF FLESH THAT DANGLE UNDER THE BEAK. THEIR SIZE AND COLOR VARY BY BREEDS AND SEX.

El Jannah
David Matthews

Chicken shops—restaurants focusing on rotisserie chicken, salads, and fries, primarily for takeaway—occupy a sacred place in Australian culture. They provide something for everyone: the busy mom picking up a whole chicken in a foil bag for an easy dinner; the greasy-fingered teenager snacking on chicken-salt-loaded fries while waiting for the school bus; tired commuters looking for a chicken-stuffed bread roll after a long day at work. Their ubiquity makes them indispensable: chicken shops are neighborhood hubs that are remarkably reliable for a good meal.

Many are also examples of immigrant ingenuity. El Jannah, in Sydney's western suburbs, is a chicken shop with a Lebanese flair. Here the chicken is butterflied, marinated, and cooked on a spit over a pile of coals. The birds are pulled off the spit once the skin is charred but the meat is still juicy, then snipped into pieces and served with flatbread, a big dollop of *toum* (like aioli, but with extra garlic and no egg), and super-salty pickled turnip and cucumber.

You can find plenty of places serving this exact combination, but the original El Jannah is the best of the bunch. Their chicken is as good as anywhere else, the pickles are sharper than others, and the toum more robust, but the atmosphere of the place is what makes it so special: the sheer number of people packed into tables, the excitement of the queue, the smoke billowing from the rooftop, and the way you're assaulted with the smell of blackened skin, fat, and charcoal as you emerge from the train station, before the restaurant even comes into sight.

El Jannah
4-8 South Street
Granville, Sydney, Australia

> HENS UNDER ONE YEAR OLD ARE CALLED PULLETS

> THERE ARE NINE DIFFERENT TYPES OF COMBS.

Torito
Kee Byung-keun

Nestled among the sushi counters that abut the inner market at Tsukiji is the matchbook-sized Torito. The counter-service restaurant specializes in chicken—in particular, *oyakodon,* which translates roughly as parent-and-child rice bowl. Chunks of chicken are braised in shoyu- and mirin-seasoned dashi, then coated in beaten eggs, which are simmered until they're just set but still fluid enough that the whole amalgam—sauce, chicken, and eggs now one—can be poured over a bowl of rice. Each spoonful feels generous and restorative. I hear Carole King singing "Chicken Soup with Rice" and see Maurice Sendak's animations dancing around my bowl as I shovel it down.

Torito is not a one-trick pony: the *tori meshi,* or chicken over rice, is an elevation of the saucy chicken and rice you've eaten elsewhere. The sauce, which most readily identifies the dish, is the least important player. The version most people outside of Japan know is dripping with a cloying, syrupy glaze; here the sauce is restrained—just sweet enough to be delicious but not distracting. It is the seasoning, not the star, and it allows the real marquee attractions of high-quality poultry and crispy skin to strut across center stage.

And every dish (including the excellent *karaage,* or fried chicken, which you can get in a set lunch or as an addition to something else) is accompanied by a cup of *torigara* soup, a palliative broth of chicken with cabbage and not much else. When the temperature gets low or when life is just unusually unkind, torigara is there for you. If only it were easier to eat there—like everywhere else in Tsukiji, it's open only through lunch, and once you're there, it's not a relaxing experience. It's cramped, crowded, and a little hectic. It's not where your tour group is going to park for a leisurely lunch. But it's where you go to take a break. Rest comes later, after you eat the rest of the market.

Torito
Tsukiji Market, Building #8, 5-2-1
Chuo-ku, Tokyo, Japan

Maganda Restaurant
Michael Solomonov

In Hebrew, their name sounds elegant: *pargiyot,* which translates to baby chickens. They're what fancy chefs call *poussins* and busy line cooks call pouss, but in almost every kebab shop (or *shipudiya*) I've been to in Israel, they use the term pargiyot. The best come on skewers, marinated in onion and garlic, salted and paprika'd, and cooked about an inch over blazing charcoal.

Maganda Restaurant, in the Yemenite Quarter of Tel Aviv (conveniently located within striding distance of Shuk Ha'Carmel, a market that sells absolutely everything), is known for their *al ha'esh* ("on the fire" or grilled) dishes. Their pargiyot—so tender and fat, stained with spice and sweetness from the lingering charcoal smoke—is so incredibly delicious, you would never believe it's just thigh meat cut into small pieces.

It's a particularly good move to go there and order both the chicken *and* the foie (yes, you heard that right—foie gras shashlik, aka foie gras on a stick). And since it's Yemeni-owned, you should probably have the Yemenite chicken soup, hummus, and a round of the salads called *salatim.*

Service is always friendly, and the space, while not terribly formal, is no longer just a living room parlor like it was when my father used to eat there in the '60s. **LP**

Maganda Restaurant
Rabbi Meir Street 26
Tel Aviv, Israel

"CHICKEN"
KELSEY WROTEN

I'VE BEEN ABSORBED BY THE IDEA THAT ALL OF MY DECISIONS THAT SEEMED SERIOUS AT THE TIME WERE ESSENTIALLY...

LATELY I'VE BEEN THINKING ABOUT IMPERMANENCE.

EVANESCENT.

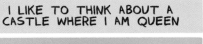

I LIKE TO THINK ABOUT A CASTLE WHERE I AM QUEEN

MY PEOPLE REJOICE.

AND ALL OF THE THINGS I'VE FORGOTTEN I DID PUT ME THERE

RIGHT NOW I FEEL LIKE A TINY SPIDER WALKING IN THE RAIN. A SINGLE DROP COULD DROWN ME.

AND WHEN I DIE I DIE WITH HONOR.

IT'S A DAMNING TRICK.

A REMINDER WE ARE TRAPPED WITHIN THE AGONY OF FORTUNE

BUT THERE IS ONE NOTION THAT MOLLIFIES.

AND RESISTANCE IS FUTILE.

Panning for Gold

"Tastes like a sponge!"
—Rob, employee

"Smells like a schoolyard!"
—Joanna, employee

By Walter Green

NOW FOR ADULTS!

FOR AGES 4-89

INCLUDES BOTH STORE-BOUGHT AND FAST FOOD VARIETIES

*Sauce Sold Separatley

What are chicken nuggets?

I know that they're eaten mostly by children, or adults who eat like children, or any people who like bite-size hunks of mechanically separated and pulverized chicken meat that are then breaded, deep-fried, and frozen for later. But what's inside their *soul*? Some parts of the Internet say nuggets usually contain a lot of fat and sometimes bits of bone and connective tissue mixed with additional hormones, additives, and chemical compounds, others say all that bad stuff you've heard is essentially exaggeration.

I had to investigate myself, so I visited the website of the National Chicken Council, which has an article called "What's Really in That Chicken Nugget?" with a section entitled "What the experts are saying." Their expert simply says, "There is no 'pink slime' in chicken nuggets." K, I didn't even know that was going to be a concern! If you want to investigate that quote, they provide a link to an interview their doctor gave to a site called Best Food Facts. I clicked the link... folks... the page was... not found. I'm assuming this guy agreed to be a mouthpiece for the Chicken Council in exchange for a lifetime supply of nuggets, got caught, and now they're trying to scrub him off the Internet entirely. (Note: Can we insert a GIF here of this doctor turning around all surprised, and his face is covered in nugget crumbs and ranch dressing?) Wait, am I a conspiracy theorist now?

Moving on, I Googled "who invented the chicken nugget" and learned about a poultry scientist named Dr. Robert C. Baker who first proposed the idea of a breaded "chicken stick" to his colleagues at Cornell University in 1963. If I was a chicken scientist and I invented, like, the holy grail of chicken technology, guess what, dawg—I'm *retirin'*. But not this guy! He dedicated his entire life to playing God of Chicken. In fact, he and his team pioneered over fifty chicken abominations, including chicken dogs, chicken hash, chicken baloney, chicken steak, and chicken ham. They also helped to develop chicken deboning machines and different mixtures to help bind pulverized chicken into different shapes. I'm assuming by this point that the man once saw his one true love pecked to death.

Turns out Dr. Baker *did* grow up on a chicken farm, and seems sincerely traumatized! He told the *New York Times,* "We'd chop the head off the chicken and it would bounce around the yard and lay there for a while before we picked it up; then we'd scoop it into a pail, and it would lie in the house a bit before my mother would get around to cooking it. Probably it did taste different. But do you want to put up with that to get the taste?"

I've never cut off the head of a chicken, nor seen it happen in real life. Anytime I've even dealt with a whole store-bought chicken, it's been impossible for me to look at its sad dead body with its sad dead skin and not imagine the life it led, and how it kind of reminds me of my cute little dog, especially when I cradle it in my arms. Pretty soon I'm like, *Is it really right that we kill these noble creatures just to cook and eat them?* I'm in a full-blown existential panic over the nature of man and right and wrong. Dr. Robert C. Baker wanted to spare us all from that, so he thought, *To hell with it, man, let's shape these things into dinosaurs.*

You can probably guess the other key player that helped shape the nugget as we now know it: McDonald's. The McNugget is likely the world's most visible nugget. It started as an experiment in their test kitchens in the late '70s as a response to our nation's nascent concerns about eating beef, and with supply coming in from Tyson Foods, the nuggets were introduced to menus and Happy Meals in 1983. Tyson still supplies McDonald's with their nuggets today, though in 2015 Tyson had to sever ties with one of its poultry farmers after a video leaked of workers stabbing and crushing chickens to death.

I called Tyson's consumer service line, where I asked a woman named Emily about what exactly goes into these morsels. "We've always used whole muscle in our nuggets," she told me. A representative from Perdue Foods (Regina) stuck to the company line as well, and said that if I *was* calling to report finding a bone or something in my chicken, they would have to find out which plant it came from, then that plant would be investigated. When I asked her about the possibility of other chicken companies maybe using that weird stuff, she decisively told me that she couldn't speak for other companies. Then I said, "Damn it, Regina, put me on the line with someone who can! Hell, get me the president of the Chicken Council if you have to! I need to know how far this thing goes!"

Just kidding. Anyways, let's start the taste test. About half were eaten dry, to get a clear sense of the flavor and quality of breading. The rest were eaten recreationally with a variety of sauces and preparation styles.

KEY:

★ TASTES PRETTY GOOD WITH LOTS OF KETCHUP ON IT

🐾 I FED A LITTLE BIT OF THIS TO MY DOG, DON'T HATE ME FOR THAT

🌱 VEGETARIAN

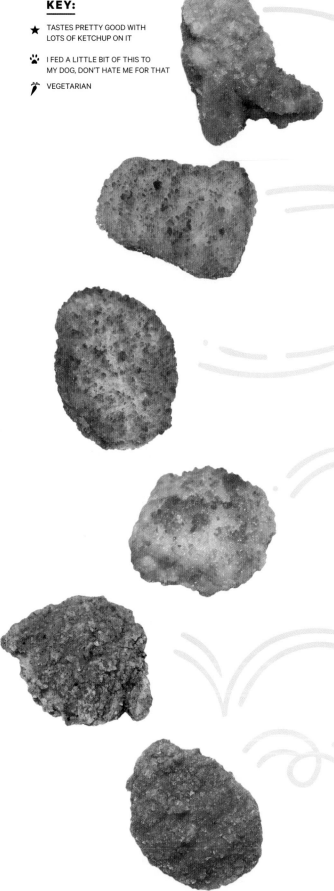

Perdue Fun Shapes ★

I microwaved these in the *Lucky Peach* office, where the idea of chicken nuggets was well received—their smell alone transported one employee Joanna back to her school-yard days—but the eating was not. Some buzzwords I heard from the millennials: mushy, bland—another employee Rob compared the experience to "biting into a wet sponge."

My main complaint? These dinosaur-shaped nuggets look like clinically depressed and severely overweight Pokémon. I don't want to body shame, but if you were a scientist at Jurassic Park and you made a T. rex that looked like this, you'd immediately be fired and laughed out of the park. If these dinosaurs had roamed the earth back in the day, I'm sure they would have been bullied by even the smallest dinosaur and later died in an extremely non-badass way, like heart failure.

Perdue Chicken Breast Nuggets ★

The flavor of these is okay, but the texture is not enjoyable at all: there's simply too much not-great breading. So there's just a lot more nugget area that will become mushy and compromise an otherwise potentially good nugget! And once a good nugget's gone bad, it's gone forever.

Perdue Whole Grain Breaded Chicken Breast Nuggets ★ 🐾

Maybe I'm imagining it, but I think the color of these reduced-fat nuggets is duller than the others. Does reducing fat change the colors of things? I can only barely detect a difference in taste between these and the regular nuggets. So, I'm cool with reducing fat across the board! Let's get that going! They decided to stick with the same mushiness level as always.

Bell & Evans Breaded Chicken Breast Nuggets ★ 🐾

Most of the nuggets I eat are "fully cooked," which means you can leave them out to thaw on your counter and then chow down. (I have done this. Also with Totino's Pizza Rolls. I am otherwise a productive member of society.) But that's not the case with Bell & Evans: these are frozen chunks of raw chicken breast meat, and it's the consumer's responsibility to make sure they reach a safe internal temperature, which felt like a lot of pressure! They suggested twenty-five to thirty minutes in the oven, but it ended up taking around forty. The results were pretty bland. My girlfriend refused to eat them without a liberal appliqué of salt and pepper. The breading fell off the nuggets as we ate them.

Coleman Organic Breaded Chicken Breast Nuggets ★

This is a well-breaded nugget. The coating looks like what you'd see at a Popeyes: a nice burnt-umber color, crispy, almost jagged. Their chicken taste lingers in the mouth, and becomes faintly medicinal. The package recommends that you eat this product with fresh fruit or organic applesauce, or consider pairing it with carrots and celery. These recipes sound like they were excerpted from a book called *Disappointing Meals for Latchkey Kids*.

Tyson Chicken Breast Nuggets ★

Over 130,000 pounds of Tyson chicken nuggets were recalled this year due to the possibility of "foreign matter contamination." But let's focus on the positives. Their light breading is ideal. For the most part, it's well adhered to the bird piece, but there are also extra crumbly bits that collect at the bottom of the bag. I always like to pour those crumbs on top of the nuggets. The Tyson coating also remains very crisp during the cooking process, but that's balanced with extreme greasiness: every bite releases a deposit of oil in your mouth. The package suggests you make a creamy honey-mustard sauce to accompany the nuggets. I'm speaking from experience when I say that no one who is eating frozen nuggets wants to take the time to make their own creamy honey-mustard sauce. They're happy to dip into whatever liquid is closest to their nuggets during snack time.

Tyson Fun Nuggets ★ 🐾

These dinosaurs are much better shaped than Perdue's. But why does fun = dinosaur? Is the goal to trick children into believing that they're eating dinosaur meat? I can think of thousands of shapes that are just as much fun, if not *more fun*, than dinosaurs. Pizza, hearts, turtles, the thumbs-up symbol. Give me a trapezoid! Shape aside, these taste somehow better than the regular Tyson nuggets. A little less grainy. Also: on Thanksgiving night, I cooked some of these in a tray with the drippings from my "bird" and I was like... I am a chef de cuisine.

Applegate Chicken Nuggets ★ 🐾

These are very tiny and ball shaped. The innards are shredded and dry, and the taste is bland. I can't imagine that anyone likes them. I think most of their sales must come from people who were hoping to buy an entirely different brand of nugget, but their store didn't have that kind, so they think, *Okay, sure, I'll get these.* Then later, that person has a conversation with their spouse and the spouse says, *Honey, let's not get those again, okay?*

Quorn Chik'n Nuggets ★ 🐾 🥕

No, fellow nü-metal fans, these vegetarian nuggets have nothing to do with the seminal group KoЯn. I'm rooting for this nugget, mainly because I play in a well-regarded Bay Area KoЯn tribute band, QoЯn. These are a bit grayer in color than the other nuggets, but they prominently display their seasoning: little salt bits are visible, and pepper peppers the interior nugget landscape. I take my first bite without reading the label too much. It has an extremely deep vegetal taste to me. Quorn says that their products are made up mostly of mycoproteins. And as soon as I read that, I think, *These do sort of taste like fungus!* But no chickens died for them that I know of, so... that's a positive.

MorningStar Farms Chik'n Nuggets ★ 🐾 🥕

These nugs are for people who love junk food, then stop eating meat for whatever reason, but who make no effort to introduce vegetables or anything healthy into their diets, so they keep eating vegetarian versions of familiar junk food. Their flavor, much like the cool word they use for chicken, is pretty close to chicken, but a little off. They're a bit mushy. They're a little salty. Fooducate, a site that grades food on their health levels, gives them a C minus. (For reference, most of the other nuggets I've tried today range from C minus to B minus.) Somebody investigate if Fooducate is in cahoots with the Chicken Council!

Nice! Chicken Nuggets ★ 🐾

This is a brand I know very well. I am getting no money to say this (but I'm open to it, *wink wink*), but there have been days where I've eaten packages of these EXCLUSIVELY. I think they taste great—and thought it might be the comfort of the familiar that made me think that—but my girlfriend (a healthy person) confirmed that they do taste very good. High marks across the board. As I continued to chew, nugget after nugget, I began to forget all about the taste test. Everything melted away, in fact. There was no drama about what might possibly be in the nugget, or any concerns for health risks. For a second, there was no Donald Trump. There was only... beautiful nugget taste. Then I bit into a tiny piece of cartilage-like substance and spat everything out.

McDonald's Chicken McNuggets ★

You know these nuggets. They're satisfying to eat—I can plow through six in under a minute and routinely regret not getting a twenty pack. They're moist, with good flavor. Also, you have to admit that McDonald's sauces are delicious. (Please take a moment to e-mail or tweet at me to admit this.) As for the shape, I've learned that McDonald's has four precut forms they use for their nuggets: the ball, the bell, the bowtie, and the boot. I'm not trying to be weird but I feel like all the ones I got during my taste test looked like misshapen genitalia.

Burger King Chicken Nuggets ★

This might have been a bad batch, but they tasted like they'd just been defrosted. The breading is too thick. The meat is chewy. The taste varies from nugget to nugget, from bland to kind of okay. My theory is that Burger King once accidentally placed an extraordinarily large order of nuggets from their nugget factory in the '90s—trillions of nuggets—and they're still trying to cook their way through that batch today.

Burger King Chicken Fries ★

This isn't high praise, but these are so much better than the nuggets. The breading is more visually appealing and better seasoned. The flavor is tangier, and the chicken is less dry. My only complaint: Why don't they call these chicken fingers? They look more like fingers made out of chicken than anything on the planet. I have an idea, Burger King: take your chicken fries and smoosh them into nugget form. Problem solved. Next! (Also, this is unrelated but why aren't pork nuggets a thing? And pork fingers?)

7-Eleven Chicken Dippers ★

Dippers look like fried testicles, and that's not me trying to be funny, that's me trying to report accurately. Why don't we call these Chicken Nutz? Why am I better at naming chicken products than every brand? These aren't very good. They're pretty, pretty dry. But if you're a frequent customer at 7-Eleven, you're probably okay with these. As a regular there myself, I feel like I should mention that the company sells their own brand of frozen chicken nuggets that I used to enjoy in my personal life when I worked across the street from one of their stores. I made conversation with the cashier at 7-Eleven about them, and she had no idea what I was talking about. I'm not happy to know more about 7-Eleven-brand products than 7-Eleven employees.

Wendy's Chicken Nuggets ★

The system for picking up my order at this Wendy's was all over the place. Sometimes numbers were being called out, sometimes names, sometimes initials, and sometimes they would just describe the contents of the order! I can't manage this kind of chaos in my life! My girlfriend had high hopes for these nuggets and fond memories of eating them in the past. She was disappointed that they weren't as good as she remembered them. Nothing ever is, folks! They started out tasty and a lot like real chicken, but ended on a bitter note. They are quite juicy. Are you tired yet of hearing about the moistness levels of nuggets?

Wendy's Spicy Chicken Nuggets ★

These are a bit thinner than the regular Wendy's nugget, but outwardly much more appealing. They've got a nice reddish-orange color to them—that's how you know something is going to be spicy nowadays. Wendy's claims these get their "kick from a special mix of black pepper, red pepper, chili pepper, and mustard seed." But these nuggets barely have a lift of the foot!! There's a hint of spiciness, but overall these aren't much better than (or even different from) their normal counterparts. I completely covered my final nuggets in ranch, barbecue sauce, and ketchup. Yes, dear reader, it did taste quite good.

Chick-fil-A Nuggets

If you thought the ethics of enjoying chicken nuggets were murky before, wait until you consider enjoying them from a company that's donated millions of dollars to anti-LGBTQ causes! These are made from cuts of white breast meat, not the chicken slurry I've shoveled down for almost every other nugget on this list, and they're indeed a little higher in quality. Even though they're slightly greasy, they may be the best fast-food nuggets on the market. They are moist. The breading is lightly and perfectly applied. And they taste quite flavorful. But like my man Dr. Robert C. Baker asked, what are we willing to put up with to get the taste? Will you let your beheaded ethics run around the yard before getting stuffed into a bucket just for a better nugget?

Carl's Jr. Chicken Stars

I haven't tried these. When the company's anti–minimum wage, pro-robot employee CEO, Andy Puzder, was tapped to be the secretary of labor in Trump's administration, I reached out to Carl's on Twitter and asked them to mail me some. As of press time, I have received ZERO envelopes full of chicken stars. But I'm gonna go ahead and assume they taste like everything having to do with our president: cheap and toxic, with an aftertaste that can only be described as un-American. Please don't @ me. **LP**

@waltergreens

How to Make *Mezcal with a Chicken Breast*

By Jim Meehan

Photographs by
Gabriele Stabile

After first traveling to Oaxaca in 1970, artist Ron Cooper began bringing jugs of mezcal from his favorite producers north to share with friends. One of those friends was fellow artist Ken Price, who drew the bottle labels when Cooper launched the import firm Del Maguey, Single Village Mezcal, in 1995.

Bottles of Del Maguey are liquid impressions of the people and places Ron represents in Oaxaca. Perhaps the most legendary is the rare *pechuga*—fewer than 2,400 bottles a year are imported into the U.S.—that he brings in from Florencio "Don Lencho" Laureano Carlos Sarmiento and his son Luis Carlos Vasquez, who distill their mezcal in a clay-and-bamboo still from roasted *espadín* agaves crushed in a millstone in the village of Santa Catarina Minas.

Between November and January, when wild mountain fruits are ripe, they fill the still with one hundred liters of their double-distilled mezcal and add about 220 pounds of apples, plums, red plantains, pineapples, almonds, and uncooked white rice, which is sewn into a cloth bag. A bone-in, skinless chicken breast is strung up above the boil (below the condenser), and the mezcal is distilled a third time. Upon completion, the breast—literally "pechuga" (which looks like chicken jerky at this point)—is removed from the still and placed in the family altar room in front of the family saints.

The first bottles of pechuga trickled into the United States in 1999. When the Mexican denomination-of-origin rules for mezcal came into effect in 1994, the production process for pechuga wasn't recognized. Cooper spent three years persuading the regulators to include it, preparing letters guaranteeing the safety of the process and flying Mexico's head veterinarian to draw blood from the chickens. Two weeks and two bottles of pechuga after the vet visit, the bureaucrats signed off.

Pechuga, interestingly, is not *always* made with chicken. Ron has a Spanish book on *pulque* (a beverage made from fermenting the sap of the agave plant) from the 1950s that mentions a pechuga from the tequila region made with a baby goat breast tossed into the liquid during the second distillation. My personal favorite is a mezcal made in Don Lencho's *palenque* (distillery) with a leg of *jamón ibérico* used in place of the chicken breast. The idea came from chef Ruben Garcia of the restaurant Minibar in Washington, D.C., who air-shipped Cooper a leg to persuade Don Lencho to try it.

Steve Olson, a sommelier who's preached the gospel of mezcal since the late nineties (and is now a partner in Del Maguey) told me, "I know of other versions made with rabbit, turkey, venison, and we even tasted one (from yet another state, Guerrero) made with venison... *and iguana*!"

No Iguanas Were Harmed in the *Making* of these *Tasting Notes*

By Peter Meehan

Del Maguey, Single Village Mezcal, Pechuga

The nose starts warm, with the smoky aroma of a tire fire—a classic mezcal thing. But this is a truly captivating expression of it: this is a fire you want to warm yourself near, smoke you'll let billow over you and soak into your clothes and think good things about in the morning when you smell it in your hair. The smoke lets up and reveals a lush, vegetal side, like stepping into a palm-crowded room at a conservatory. Faint notes of citrus and gasoline accompany the first sip, when you realize how well this mezcal drinks. It's fleet-footed but powerful; it swings a sledgehammer of flavor with a surgeon's precision. Hard to resist.

Don Amado Pechuga

The aromas of the Don Amado are there, and then they're gone. It starts with something citrusy—but it's smelling the wax from supermarket citrus on your hands after putting away the groceries. The petrol note is remembering what the pump smells like a few minutes after pulling out of the station. (I am a person, I should note, who likes the smell of gasoline.) There are flowers, and something like wet stone. Sipping it, I found it oily, grassy, smooth, and long, with a sweet finish that had the tiniest vanilla kiss-off. A pechuga that'd be fine to pass the hours with.

Mezcal Tosba Pechuga

Aromas of Band-Aids dominate the nose of this turkey mezcal, but they eventually give way to appealing notes of mesquite. It sips hot—even at a relatively low proof—with a tobacco-y, medicinal finish. A pechuga for those already initiated in the ways of mezcal.

Mezcal Real Minero Pechuga

The nose is conversational: open and generous, with echoes of stone fruit and reflections of dried fruit. It peaks with a hit of spring break: suntan lotion, pineapples, bright banana-peel notes. Maybe a little note of chocolate—more milk chocolate or cocoa mix than that spice-laden Mexican chocolate. On the palate it is spicy and peppery, with a short moment of dusty spice cabinet and a surprising but pleasant maple-caramel surge at the end. This is least smoky of any of the mezcals in the tasting; it drinks easy even at 51.7% alcohol by volume.

El Jolgorio Mezcal Pechuga

Like breathing in apricots and then, all of a sudden, burying your head in a plant after it rains. I thought I smelled bananas, but am *I* bananas? (My wife, Hannah, smells the pechuga and she says I am right. I am not satisfied, worrying that the power of suggestion has corrupted her perception. Later I read that plantains went in the still.) Maybe a note of vanilla. Can I say apricot kernels without seeming weird? It's bright and beguiling, but then you sip it and the sun sets on the tropical daydream, and it turns to smoke and Band-Aids in the mouth. **LP**

Label Literacy

By Joanna Sciarrino
Illustration by Stephen Lurvey

Growing up, my uncle Lenny had a pet rooster called Gregory. Gregory ate corn and roamed around freely in the backyard of their house in Woodside, Queens. When Gregory was old and big enough, my great-uncle Cosmo killed him and cooked him for dinner. I don't know how Gregory tasted, but I do know that no one wondered where he came from, how he was treated, or whether he had been pumped full of steroids. But today there are lots of questions to answer about how a chicken lived and died: Was it allowed outside? Was it fed antibiotics? What does it mean that it's "organic"? Here's a guide to what all those labels mean—and which matter—to boost your chicken-buying acumen.

Air Chilled: After processing, chickens need to be rapidly chilled to prevent the spread of salmonella and other stuff you don't want to eat. Most birds are water cooled—submerged in circulating tanks of cold water that's often treated with chlorine or hydrogen peroxide. Critics say this method causes chickens to absorb water, which dilutes their flavor. Air-chilled birds are passed through several chambers of cold air until they reach a safe temperature, and we find that they tend to be better tasting, if more expensive.

All-Vegetable Diet: Chickens who go meat-free get this label. Others are given corn- and soybean-based feed that includes animal by-products, which are described thusly by the Animal Welfare Institute: "unused parts of other animals, for example meat and bone meal, feather meal, and/or manure, eggs, and hatchery waste." Yum.

Amish Country/Amish Raised: This term is not regulated by the USDA, so technically anyone can use it. Extra points for authenticity if there's an image of a little horse-drawn buggy on the package.

Antibiotic Free/No Antibiotics Ever/Raised without Antibiotics: Most chicks that will be raised for meat receive a preemptive dose of antibiotics. (Don't be all Jenny McCarthy judgy; medicine isn't all bad.) Chickens raised without that first-day dose, or any other subsequent doses, can be labeled "no antibiotics ever" or "raised without antibiotics."

"Antibiotic free" is not a USDA-approved label, but it implies that the birds have gone through an antibiotic withdrawal period of seven to fourteen days before slaughter, so there are no traces of medicine left in their system.

Cage Free: Unlike big-industry egg-laying birds, which are kept in cages, broiler chickens are almost always kept together in growing houses, sheds, or barns. By the USDA definition, cage free just means birds can roam around freely in an enclosed area, but not outdoors like free-range birds, so this label doesn't really mean anything.

Enhanced Chicken Products: Like your chicken with a little extra flavor? Enhanced chickens have been pumped with things like salt, sugar, or a "broth-like solution." If you opt for these birds, which you shouldn't, the ingredient list will give you a rundown of the enhancements that have been performed. You may also see this as "basted" or "self basted."

raising, handling, and slaughtering animals—but they'll all help you sleep better than what the USDA expects out of standard chicken handling.

Kosher: Slaughtered by a *shohet*, a trained butcher under rabbinical supervision. The shohet blesses the bird and uses an unblemished knife in one swift movement to sever the trachea, esophagus, and major blood vessels. The chicken is inverted over a bucket and left until the blood is drained. The lungs are then inspected; damaged lungs disqualify the bird for kosher certification. The birds are soaked in clean water, dried, salted, and then washed again before packaging.

Made in the USA: You guessed it: per the Country of Origin Labeling law (which the government refers to as COOL), chickens with this label are hatched, raised, and processed in the U.S.

Natural: Anything added to these chickens must be natural (not artificial, like chemical preservatives or coloring agents). This term also implies minimal processing. Either way, labels must include a statement explaining how it's natural.

No GMOs: The USDA does not yet have a standard for disclosing genetic modification on labels, but third-party organizations can verify non-GMO products. The Non-GMO Project has one of the most prevalent and strict labels, but even their chicken feed can still contain up to 0.9 percent genetically modified crops, so it's not really none.

No Hormones Added: The USDA prohibits the use of hormones in chicken production, so all chickens are hormone-free chickens and this label doesn't mean anything. Growth drugs and antibiotics, however, are totally fine in a "no hormones added" chicken.

Organic: To be certified organic, chickens must be raised and processed by the following USDA guidelines and checked by a certifying agent:
– chickens must be fed certified-organic feed (grown without the use of pesticides or chemicals and containing no animal by-products, antibiotics, or GMOs)
– chickens cannot receive drugs, including antibiotics and hormones but not including vaccinations
– chickens must have access to the outdoors (see: Free Range)

Pastured: Though not an official USDA label, "pasture-raised" chickens are able to roam and forage on grass, seeds, insects, and so on during the day, but are kept enclosed at night.

Retained Water: Any reported water weight absorbed by the chickens during the post-slaughter chilling process, as required by the USDA. You will find this listed as a percentage (ranging from 8 to 12), or sometimes as "added moisture," but 0 percent or "no retained water" is preferable. This is mostly found on fresh chicken, which often has some extra liquid in the package. **LP**

Farm Raised: All chickens grown for food are raised on some sort of farm, so this label can be used for any chicken, no matter how terrifying the "farm."

Free Range/Free Roaming: Chickens raised in climate-controlled growing houses with access to the outdoors or some sort of fenced-in area qualify for this label. We'd say it's good, but not great. Free range does not mean the birds can forage freely or that they are organic.

Fresh: The meat has never been frozen.

Halal: Killed by a Muslim butcher according to *dhabihah*, the guidelines for proper slaughter under Islamic law. The chicken must be blessed before the throat and arteries are cut from front to back with a very sharp, undamaged blade. The blood is then drained from the body, as the chicken must be completely dead before post-slaughter processing can begin.

Humane/Humanely Raised: Humane treatment isn't regulated by the USDA, so for this to actually mean something, it has to be verified by a third party; look for labels like "certified humane" or "animal welfare approved." Each organization has its own standards for

COUNTING OUR CHICKENS

1 2 3 4 5 6 7 8 9

THE GLOBAL CHICKEN industry is so vast it almost defies comprehension.

The broiler chicken—the industry term for a chicken raised for meat—is far and away the most common live-stock animal. The Food and Agriculture Organization of the United Nations estimates that **60 billion** chickens are killed annually for meat.

By Tamara Micner

ANIMALS SLAUGHTERED IN 2014

62 billion — CHICKENS
2.9 billion — DUCKS
1.5 billion — PIGS
1.1 billion — RABBITS
0.6 billion — TURKEYS
0.5 billion — SHEEP
0.4 billion — GOATS
0.3 billion — COWS

In other words, on average about

1,966

chickens are slaughtered every second for meat.

In 2014 there were roughly **three times** as many chickens on earth as humans at any given moment.

CHICKENS:
21,409,683,000

HUMANS:
7,167,884,000

MEAT PRODUCTION IN METRIC TONS (2014)

PORK:
115,313,734

CHICKEN:
100,352,826

BEEF:
64,681,068

LAMB AND MUTTON:
8,960,335

TURKEY:
5,611,054

GOAT:
5,524,075

DUCK:
4,331,381

RABBIT:
1,559,927

Chicken accounts for roughly **33 percent** of global meat production by weight. Globally, only pork is more popular than chicken.

In the United States, chicken has been the most popular meat since the early nineties.

PER CAPITA MEAT CONSUMPTION IN THE UNITED STATES

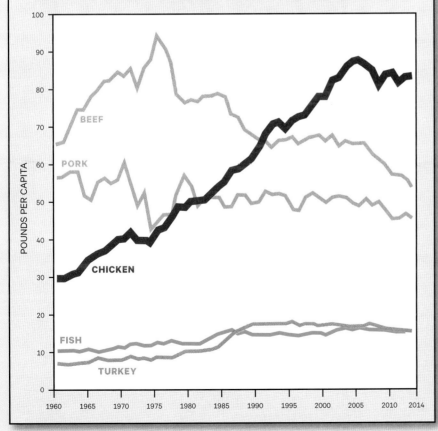

POUNDS PER CAPITA

BEEF

PORK

CHICKEN

FISH

TURKEY

100
90
80
70
60
50
40
30
20
10
0

1960 1965 1970 1975 1980 1985 1990 1995 2000 2005 2010 2014

The average American eats **84.1 pounds** of chicken a year, the equivalent of about **32 birds**.

The worldwide average is **25.6 pounds**.

This massive scale is enabled in large part by advances in chicken breeding: the modern broiler is a marvel of agricultural technology.

The average bird is larger,

AVERAGE WEIGHT AT SLAUGHTER

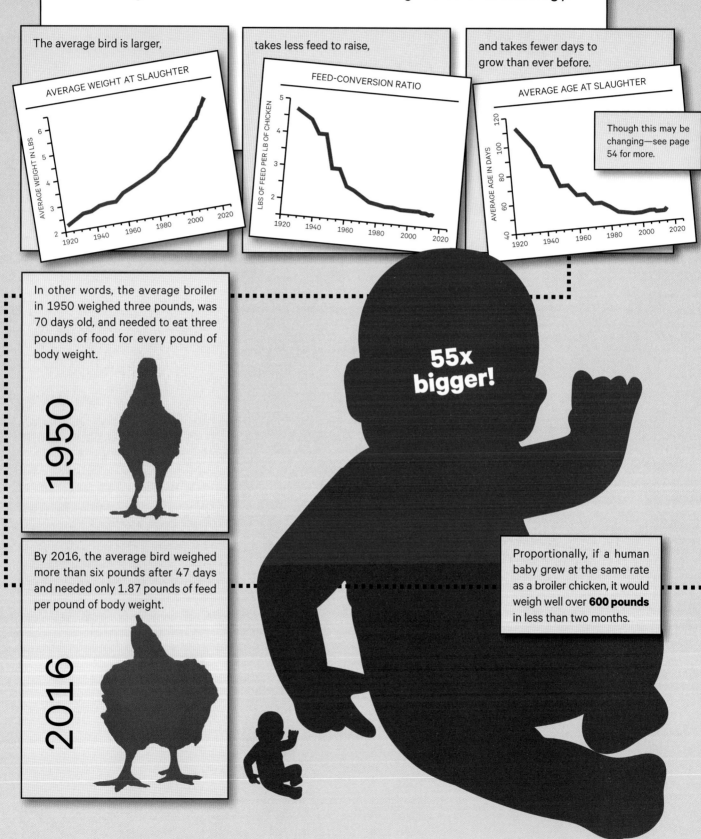

takes less feed to raise,

FEED-CONVERSION RATIO

and takes fewer days to grow than ever before.

AVERAGE AGE AT SLAUGHTER

Though this may be changing—see page 54 for more.

In other words, the average broiler in 1950 weighed three pounds, was 70 days old, and needed to eat three pounds of food for every pound of body weight.

1950

55x bigger!

By 2016, the average bird weighed more than six pounds after 47 days and needed only 1.87 pounds of feed per pound of body weight.

2016

Proportionally, if a human baby grew at the same rate as a broiler chicken, it would weigh well over **600 pounds** in less than two months.

Chicken production leads to pollution with local and global consequences.

Much of the local pollution is attributable to chicken manure, which is valuable as fertilizer and is sometimes even burned for power generation, but also often leaks into the surrounding area and contributes to water contamination with nitrogen, phosphorus, heavy metals, and antibiotics.

Each chicken produces around 2.5 pounds of manure, which adds up to 150 billion pounds for the earth to absorb every year. That much chicken shit weighs about as much as **205 Empire State Buildings**.

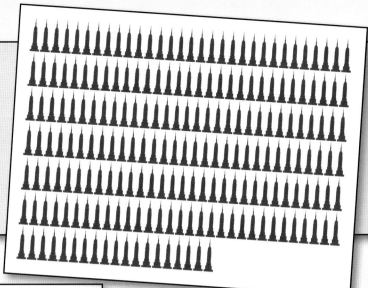

Globally, the FAO estimates that livestock production is responsible for **14.5 percent** of total human-caused greenhouse gas emissions...

LIVESTOCK GREENHOUSE GAS EMISSIONS

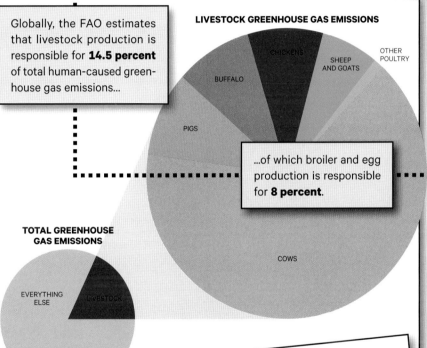

CHICKENS
SHEEP AND GOATS
OTHER POULTRY
BUFFALO
PIGS
COWS

...of which broiler and egg production is responsible for **8 percent**.

TOTAL GREENHOUSE GAS EMISSIONS

EVERYTHING ELSE
LIVESTOCK

So it's true that chicken is less carbon intensive than other meats...

CARBON FOOTPRINT OF MEATS

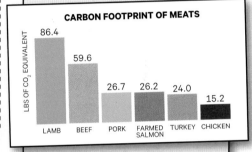

LBS OF CO$_2$ EQUIVALENT

LAMB	BEEF	PORK	FARMED SALMON	TURKEY	CHICKEN
86.4	59.6	26.7	26.2	24.0	15.2

...but much more carbon intensive than other foods.

CARBON FOOTPRINT OF OTHER FOODS

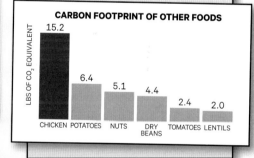

LBS OF CO$_2$ EQUIVALENT

CHICKEN	POTATOES	NUTS	DRY BEANS	TOMATOES	LENTILS
15.2	6.4	5.1	4.4	2.4	2.0

And the world's demand for chicken is projected to continue growing faster than the human population in the coming decades. **LP**

HUMAN POPULATION VS. CHICKEN CONSUMPTION

HUMAN POPULATION (BILLIONS)

CHICKEN CONSUMPTION (METRIC TONS)

150M

100M

50M

0

10
9
8
7
6
5
4
3

PROJECTED

1961 1967 1973 1979 1985 1991 1997 2003 2009 2015 2021

SOURCES: FAO, USDA, OECD, The Environmental Group, National Chicken Council

Cock Fight

Pitting the planet's most distinctive
chickens against each other

BRESSE GAULOISE

"The queen of poultry, the poultry of kings"
—*Jean Anthelme Brillat-Savarin*

FROM FRANCE
SIGNATURE: AN AOC LABEL
RARITY: 1.2 MILLION/YEAR
PRICE: $20–$100/BIRD
FEATURED IN: *POULARDE EN VESSIE*

Anyone can make sparkling wine, but champagne can come only from a specific region. And anyone can raise a chicken, but only certain chickens raised in Bourg-en-Bresse carry the AOC label. They live outdoors, with at least one hundred square feet of their own space (bigger than my first NYC bedroom), and are encouraged to forage for bugs and grasses (healthier than my first meals while fending for myself). And they are monitored by the Centre de Sélection de la Volaille de Bresse to ensure everything is up to AOC standards. Chef Daniel Boulud describes it as "a beauty of a bird, which is monitored from birth until it reaches your plate. It feeds on maize, seeds, insects, and worms. You can really see the difference this makes when you look at the liver and fat. The color of the liver is whiter, and the fat is much more yellow, showing its better diet. This is also a walking chicken, so the legs are as devéloped as the breast. It takes longer to cook, because it's a sturdy bird, but the payoff is there. Where I grew up, outside Lyon, we would buy the *poulets de Bresse* live from the market and then grow them further on our farm, until we were ready to eat them. I'm not sure that complied with the AOC guidelines, but I like to think my father did a nice job with them. They certainly tasted fantastic."

CORNISH CROSS

"The chicken in every pot"

FROM THE UNITED STATES
SIGNATURE: UBIQUITY
RARITY: 50 BILLION/YEAR
FEED CONVERSION RATIO: 1.6
AGE TO MATURITY: 6 WEEKS
FEATURED IN: EVERY BUCKET OF THE
COLONEL'S ORIGINAL RECIPE

Young chickens slaughtered for meat are referred to as "broilers." And no breed converts feed into meat better than the Cornish Cross (a hybrid of the Cornish breed from England and the White Rock variety of the American Plymouth Rock). Originally intended to be a fighter, the Cornish somehow lost a lot of the aggression that its parents had. What it gained, though, was a muscular, flavorful body that could be harvested young, which paired well with the Plymouth Rock that was popular in New England for its juicy meat and ease of rearing. When you go to the grocery store for that shrink-wrapped tray of skinless breasts or grab a box of chicken nuggets from the drive-through, chances are you benefitted from these birds' freakishly fast ability to turn the brutish and short span of their lives into fluffy, dry white meat.

By Ryan Harrington   *Illustrations by Maria Chimishkyan*

PLEASE DO NOT FEED THE CHICKENS

JERSEY GIANT

"The supersized bird"

FROM THE UNITED STATES
SIGNATURE: LARGE SIZE
WEIGHT: 10–15 POUNDS
HEIGHT: 16–26 INCHES
AGE TO MATURITY: 9 MONTHS
FEATURED IN: WHOLE ROASTED CHICKEN

As its name may suggest, this breed was created in New Jersey and is HUGE. Bred in the late nineteenth century to be as large as possible, the Jersey Giant was meant to compete with the turkey as a family-feeding table bird. They can weigh three times as much as the average broiler chicken. As a heritage pure breed, they may grow slower than most commercial chickens, but that extra time develops a better flavor and texture. And just as they grow slower, the best ways to cook them are traditional slower methods. Consider it for your next Thanksgiving dinner!

AYAM CEMANI

"The Lamborghini of poultry"

FROM INDONESIA
SIGNATURE: UNRELENTING DARKNESS
FEATHERS: BLACK
SKIN: BLACK
MEAT: BLACK
ORGANS: BLACK
FEATURED IN: *HAINAN JI FAN*

Believed to have mystical powers, the Ayam Cemani is traditionally eaten for medicinal purposes or sacrificed for good fortune. Why is it so revered? This Indonesian bird is completely black, tip to tail, inside and out. This small bird needs slow, wet cooking methods—like those used to make a plate of Hainanese chicken rice—to showcase its full flavor and draw out that spiritual power. But because of low laying rates and import bans, it is hard to come by—and extremely rare in the U.S. When it first landed on American shores, its photogenic appearance and rarity made it a media star. Breeders were able to sell individual birds for as much as $2,500.

DONG TAO

"The Dragon Chicken"

FROM VIETNAM
SIGNATURE: CRAZY LEGS
LEG CIRCUMFERENCE: 4 INCHES
PRICE: $1,250/BIRD

The circumference of the thick, scaly legs of the Dong Tao can match an adult human's wrist. These giant legs are caused by an enzyme that also happens to result in sweet, tender meat. Originally bred for the royal family, this chicken is now a symbol of wealth and prosperity for all of Vietnam's elite, eaten as a delicacy in finer restaurants. It becomes especially popular during Tet, the Vietnamese New Year, when suppliers struggle, and often fail, to meet demand for this thick-legged bird.

JIDORI

"The Kobe beef of chicken"

FROM JAPAN
SIGNATURE: A LIFE OF LUXURY
DIET: WILD CLOVER, VEGETABLES, TOMATOES, AND APPLES
PRODUCTION: 1 PERCENT OF DOMESTIC MARKET
FEATURED IN: *KIRITANPO NABE* (RICE-STICK HOT POT)

Jidori means "chicken of the earth," and in Japan these birds are required by law to be free range. Raised in open pastures, they are allowed to grow slowly (up to three times longer than other chickens), to minimize their stress and ensure quality. They are slaughtered and delivered to kitchens within the same day, and are most likely the kind of chicken you'll see served raw, as sashimi. But the earthy flavor and firm texture stand up to the long-simmering waters of a fragrant hot pot, too.

SILKIE

"The teddy bear bird"

FROM CHINA
SIGNATURE: FLUFFY PLUMAGE
FEATHERS: WHITE, BLACK, BLUE, OR BUFF
SKIN: BLACKISH
EGGS: CREAM
FEATURED IN: *WU GU JI TONG* (SILKIE CHICKEN SOUP)

Unlike most other birds, the Silkie's feathers are not barbed and instead puff out. This downy "fur" is incredibly soft to the touch and makes them look much bigger than they actually are. Adding to their cute appeal, they make excellent mothers—it's been said they'll raise ducklings and goslings. And though their feathers come in a few colors, white being the most common, their flesh is always dark gray with a bluish hue. Because of this coloration, they have traditionally been seen as having medicinal properties in their native China, making them an ideal candidate for a restorative chicken soup.

KUROILER

"The rural revolutionary"

FROM INDIA
SIGNATURE: SCAVENGING
**BILL & MELINDA GATES
FOUNDATION FUNDING:** $12.4 MILLION
**PROJECTED ANNUAL
PRODUCTION:** 2 MILLION
FEATURED IN: *KUKU KIENYEJI*

Initially bred in India in the early '90s by a socially conscious entrepreneur, the Kuroiler was designed to be an excellent rural-village chicken and is even finding great purchase in Uganda, outperforming indigenous breeds. They provide more meat and eggs than other local species and are extremely efficient scavengers, adapted to live off the waste from kitchens and farms. The Bill & Melinda Gates Foundation has donated millions of dollars to fund the distribution of this breed throughout Africa, helping impoverished villages become sustainable poultry producers. These rugged birds may initially have a gamey flavor, but their long cooking time allows rich spices in stews like kuku kienyeji to permeate deep throughout the meat.

FEATHERLESS CHICKEN

"The bare-all bird"

FROM ISRAEL
SIGNATURE: NUDITY
FEATHERS: NONE!
FEATURED IN: COMING SOON TO A CHICKEN SHACK NEAR YOU

In Israel, believed to be where humanity first used chickens for food, scientists have bred a chicken without any feathers. This chicken grows leaner and faster in warm climates, because it doesn't waste the energy and calories that traditional chickens do trying to stay cool. Proponents believe it saves the chicken from having to grow feathers, which farmers have to spend time and money to pluck anyway. However, feathers help keep parasites and sunburn at bay. Still, this could be the future of mass-produced poultry in large parts of the world. Despite the lack of plumage, its flesh is reported to taste like chicken.

Tastes Like...

By Chris Cohen
Illustrations by Rob Engvall

The bouillon cube is often portrayed as a Faustian bargain struck with modern food science, wherein convenient mediocrity replaces laborious but noble simmering. This vilification isn't entirely fair. Recipes for bouillon cubes can be found in eighteenth-century European cookbooks—Escoffier made them! And the off-the-shelf version of the bouillon cube is older than your grandma: it was first developed by a Swiss inventor named Julius Maggi in 1908, and his namesake brand is still one of the world's most popular today.

So what were old-school bouillon cubes like?

One of the first written descriptions comes from Vincent La Chapelle, household chef to second-tier nobility across Europe during the eighteenth century. In his 1733 book, *The Modern Cook,* he gives a recipe for "the way of making Broth Cakes, which may be conveniently carried abroad, and preserv'd above a Year." The recipe is an old-school doozy: it calls for the reader to first make a stock from half of a large bull, a whole calf, two sheep, two dozen chickens, and twelve to fifteen pounds of staghorn, then reduce the stock into a demi-glace with a honey-like consistency, and finally dry that out in the oven. But his motivation for making them was more modern—the cakes, he wrote, are perfect for busy cooks who "have neither time nor convenience of getting the necessary ingredients."

And what about the bouillon cubes of today?

Today's bouillon cubes never exist as stock—they're compressed chunks of pre-dried powders.

It's probably not a surprise that salt is the largest component of Maggi's cubes—it accounts for over half the weight in the U.K. recipe. The second-largest portion is some sort of starch. The particular kind varies by region—Maggi uses cassava flour in West Africa, for instance, but wheat flour or cornstarch elsewhere. Dried vegetable powders, herbs, and spices are added and customized by region: France gets cilantro, pepper, and clove; the Middle East gets white pepper, turmeric, and coriander. Since 2012, iron has been added in markets that struggle with anemia. For a sense of umami, the cubes include a hit of glutamate. Sometimes this means where it occurs naturally, like in a powder made from fermented soybeans, while in other cases it's good old MSG.

But why does it taste like chicken? That's complicated. In some regions, the company is making a push toward more recognizable ingredients, using dehydrated chicken meat and chicken fat. In most of the world, though, Maggi purchases additives produced by enormous yet mysterious industrial flavoring firms. In those cases, the flavor compounds are designed to mimic the flavor of chicken—without requiring any participation from chickens themselves. What we know as "chicken" flavor is a moving target: in Europe, flavor scientists employ a formula that tastes like long-simmered chicken; in the Middle East, the flavor is amplified with more spices.

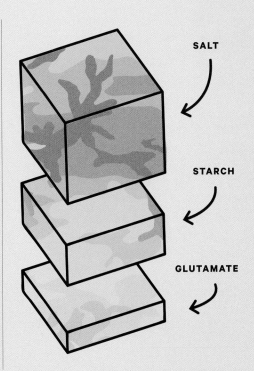

SALT

STARCH

GLUTAMATE

How are they made?

Maggi's cubes get made in big factories arranged vertically—ingredients (mostly pre-dried) are lifted to the top floor, and gravity aids each subsequent step. Ingredients are weighed out, then dropped one story down into horizontal drums, where they're homogenized and dosed with minute amounts of oil and water to aid in binding. Time is money, so careful testing has determined the bare minimum of mixing—usually just a few minutes.

The final mix is deposited into a giant bag called—seriously—the Big Bag. Each bag can weigh more than a thousand pounds. The Big Bag is then positioned over a press on the floor below.

The goal is a four-gram cube, fourteen millimeters on each side. A large rotating table of pneumatic pistons presses the powder into a mold with a carefully calibrated pressure. Too much force, and the cubes won't dissolve when the consumer is cooking with them. Too little, and the powder won't bind into a solid cube. The presses move almost too fast to register: each can produce at least sixteen cubes per second. From there, the cubes speed along a conveyor belt to the wrapping line, where a machine with speedy metal "fingers" wraps them like an endless stream of tiny Christmas presents.

Much like irritated travelers trying to catch a flight, at least some bouillon cubes need to be scanned before they're released into the world. Some are opened and visually inspected; others pass through a metal detector or an X-ray scanner to ensure no bits of metal or other contaminants ended up in the cube.

BIG BAG

Who's using all those cubes?

They've become foundational to home cooking around the world—in parts of the Middle East, Latin America, and (especially) West Africa, you can't escape bouillon. (In Central and West Africa alone, Maggi moves more than a hundred million cubes every day!) And while it doesn't come from vats of long-boiled stock these days, or even a real chicken, it's how millions of people make dishes that at least taste like it. LP

To Wash or Not to Wash?

By Harold McGee   *Illustrations by Rob Engvall*

Did you get a whiff of the chicken shitstorm of August 2013? It was a brief but intense controversy (complete with the #chickenshitstorm hashtag, bestowed by Michael Ruhlman) over a USDA-funded public-relations campaign that warned against washing raw chicken before cooking. According to the Don't Wash Your Chicken! crusade, most of the raw poultry we buy is contaminated with infectious bacteria from the animals' guts, and washing splashes those bacteria all over the kitchen, where they can contaminate other foods and utensils and end up making us sick. In other words, raw chicken is too dirty to clean safely, so we should just slide it right from package to pan with whatever stale fluids and smells come with it, kill the bacteria with the heat of cooking—and enjoy!

The initial PR blast included a press release, a YouTube "Germ-Vision Animation" that simulated toxic chicken splatter in ghoulish fluorescent green, and four short Don't Wash Your Chicken! videos and photo novellas, in which unwitting cooks were schooled and saved from washing just before they made their roast or oven-fry or stir-fry or mole. The blast had its intended effect and kicked up plenty of media gusts. NPR: "Julia Child

Was Wrong: Don't Wash Your Raw Chicken, Folks." *Slate*: "Don't Wash Your Chicken! No Matter What Your Cookbook Says." *Gizmodo*: "Science Says Not to Wash Your Chicken Before You Cook It."

These feature stories then provoked social-media winds of apocalyptic force—but in the opposite direction. Alton Brown tweeted to his (at the time) 625,000 Twitter followers a series of Post-it instructions for safe chicken preparation: after washing gently, "douse house with accelerant," "burn down house to kill germs," and "take off and nuke the entire site from orbit." On Ruhlman's website, there was a post called "Bacteria! Run Away! Run Away!"

Then an eerie calm set in. There was a follow-up "Don't Panic!" blog post from NPR and some backpedaling from the chief campaigner. As the post paraphrased Drexel University nutrition-sciences professor Dr. Jennifer Quinlan, "If you rinse your chicken out of safety concerns, just stop," she says, "because you are making it less safe. If you are doing it to enhance flavor, that's fine, but

He doesn't look at me the same, ever since I washed his chicken...

use proper precautions." This clarification, that the real problem with washing chicken is the cook's misconceived motivation for washing, suggested that the campaign motto should have been Don't Wash Your Chicken for the Wrong Reasons!

The storm passed, but without really clearing the air. Many cooks, myself included, continue to rinse chickens of old fluids and smells, to soak them in flavorful brines, massage them with butter, stuff them with herbs, and otherwise brave their bacterial load in the pursuit of deliciousness. Food-safety professionals continue to publish reports that categorize poultry washing as a food-safety "mistake." And some have gone so far as to imply the possibility of combatting public violations with lawsuits.

For a study published in the November/December 2016 issue of *Food Protection Trends,* researchers at the USDA and UC Davis scrutinized four popular TV food shows and their hosts, by name. The researchers logged the purported violations committed on camera, which included not washing hands, not washing cutting boards, licking fingers, and washing—or even mentioning the

washing of—meat or poultry. Noting first that food companies are increasingly likely to be held liable for causing illness and deaths, the study concludes: "In the future, will cooking programs also be held responsible if they fail to model safe-handling practices?" There's a food trend to follow!

That ominous escalation got me to wondering about a couple of things. First: What evidence is there that washing chickens is a significant threat to public health? And then, to turn the study's concluding sentence around: Should food-safety programs be held responsible if they fail to generate confidence and respect for their guidelines?

The evidence against chicken washing—what Science really has to say about it—turns out to be practically nonexistent. I scoured the food-safety literature for any studies of meat-washing splatter and its contribution to the risk of foodborne illness. I found not a single peer-reviewed study—just one 2003 report from Campden BRI, an independent British food-research consortium, with the title "Microbiological risk factors associated with the domestic handling of meat." To analyze the risk posed by washing, the authors covered the work surfaces around a sink with paper, coated a chicken with red food dye, washed the chicken for ten seconds, and noted that red spots appeared on the paper as far as seventy centimeters, more than two feet, from the sink.

That's it! The report includes no actual microbiology to see whether splashing water picks up bacteria and carries them in significant numbers—a real question, since half of the argument against washing is that it *doesn't* remove significant numbers of bacteria from foods. Nor does it estimate the risk splashing might pose compared to less ambiguous hazards, like handling a leaky supermarket package of raw meat, or not washing hands diligently during cooking, or using the same towel to dry clean hands and not-so-clean countertops.

To make sure that I wasn't missing something, I checked with half a dozen food-safety professionals. They generously responded with links, reports, and USDA information sheets—all of which assert the risk of washing meats, but don't cite an actual study of the risk. Dr. Donald Schaffner, a professor at Rutgers, agreed that "definitive peer-reviewed data do not seem to exist."

And I wasn't entirely convinced by that Campden BRI report. As a longtime chicken-washer, I found it hard to believe that the water flies two feet from the sink. So I replicated that simulation in my own kitchen. I calibrated the flow rate from my faucet to match the report's moderate thirty-five milliliters (about two tablespoons) per second, and put the chicken under the stream.

I did see some splashing outside the sink, but only when I held the chicken high up, almost level with the countertop, and put the faucet on spray mode so that its flow was accelerated through a couple dozen small holes. I also felt that splashing. I was standing less than a foot away from the bird, so of course my paper-coated shirt got wet with chicken rinse. Disgusting! When I did what I usually do, put the chicken on a plate at the bottom of the sink and let the water flow normally, there was no discernible splatter on the countertops or me.

My unsurprising conclusion: it's possible to wash chicken carelessly, in a way that might spread contamination onto countertops and draining boards and the cook. It's also possible to wash chicken carefully, in a way that confines its microbes largely to the sink, where other unclean things also get cleaned.

And the same is true for those other unclean things. Everything that goes into the sink, and the sink itself, can be washed carelessly or carefully. That includes hands, cutting boards, utensils, and scrubbing pads. It includes the vegetables and fruits that the food-safety pros say we *should* wash, and that are reported to be responsible for about as many annual cases of foodborne illness as meat and poultry.

It seems to me that instead of discouraging the laudable general impulse to start cooking with clean ingredients, and creating dubious categories of the should-be-washed and the unwashable, it makes much more sense to define and encourage careful washing and sink-faucet-towel work in general. And to do the definitive experiments to clarify what the real risks are, and what the best practices would be. As Dr. Schaffner at Rutgers wrote to me when he couldn't find any studies of washing, "This is a research opportunity." A big one!

The Don't Wash Your Chicken! storm offers another kind of opportunity, an obvious occasion for the food-safety community to reevaluate the way it approaches its mission. The PR campaign garnered a lot of media play and views for its videos. But it also got spectacular blowback from respected figures with millions of followers in the cooking world. Inviting that kind of mockery, and then backpedaling on the message, only deepens confusion and doubt about food safety, and diminishes the credibility of its authorities. Nor is their image likely to be improved by sitting in judgment of popular food personalities and hinting at legal action.

We absolutely do need credible sources of information, and good practical advice. Foodborne illness kills thousands of people every year, and neither the food industry nor the USDA is doing all it could and should to make the food supply cleaner. If you're not especially concerned about this, take a look at Lynne Terry's award-winning 2015 report "A Game of Chicken" in the *Oregonian*. During her investigation of several salmonella outbreaks over several years, all cases traced back to Foster Farms. In a follow-up to the story, she asked an Oregon epidemiologist for his advice on cooking chicken, and his answer was, "Treat it like hazardous waste."

Sure, it's a challenge to convince home cooks to keep invisible hazards in mind, or change daily habits, or correct misconceptions. That makes strategy especially important. Here are a few moves that have proved to be counterproductive: Misrepresent very preliminary science as settled scary fact. Discourage behavior that's rooted in an instinct for cleanliness. Caricature what cooks actually do. Make strong statements and then mostly retract them. Provoke ridicule from leaders in the community you're trying to influence.

What might be a more productive path? It seems pretty obvious: engage with people who actually cook.

The safety pros should take a break from the echo chamber of technical conferences and journals to spend time with cooking pros, chefs, and Ruhlmans and Browns. They should visit the country's best kitchens not to log violations, but to listen and learn, to understand why cooks handle food the way they do, how they think and feel about making tasty and attractive and wholesome things with their hands. They should invite collaboration on coherent, workable guidelines that the culinary pros can actually recommend to their communities.

One expert I particularly admire for his critical approach

Why doesn't my boyfriend wash my chicken?

to safety guidelines wrote to me apropos of unnecessary and risky handling, saying that "the home cook sees the leftover innards of the chicken and thinks that they have to be removed... There really is no reason to remove the intestinal organs as a part of preparing the chicken/poultry for cooking." This may be true from a strictly hygienic and nutritional point of view. But from that point of view, there's no reason for most of the things that cooks do!

Cooks may remove the innards from a chicken because they're in an inedible bag, or because they hate innards, or because they love them and want to cook them perfectly. They go to the trouble of washing chickens, brining and massaging and stuffing them and tying them up, because they seek not just to detoxify foods, but to make them as delicious as they can be. Cooks have their own good reasons, and most eaters are glad they do. **LP**

Cooks & Chefs

Ashley Christensen's insight into fried chicken
and the key to making a perfect batch.

Photographs by Gabriele Stabile

Ashley Christensen is the chef and owner of six spots in Raleigh, North Carolina, including the celebrated Poole's Diner and Beasley's Chicken + Honey, a restaurant devoted to fried chicken and all the things that go with it. Since Beasley's signature fried chicken is a multistep process that requires equipment most of us don't keep at home, we asked Ashley for some "chicken-fried" recipes instead of fried chicken ones; they follow our chicken chat below. – **Joanna Sciarrino**

I love the idea of doing one thing and doing it really well, which is why I opened Beasley's Chicken + Honey. Beasley was my mom's nickname for me as a kid; my dad was a hobbyist beekeeper, which is how we got into drizzling honey over chicken. It was something I thought belonged to our family, but it's actually an old Southern thing.

When I was growing up, my mom would get out the skillet and fry chicken every couple weeks. There's so much to experiences like that, where you don't just remember sitting down and eating chicken—I remember everything it took for my mom to get it on the table.

She cooked all the time, but whenever she fried chicken, she didn't do it right before dinner with this goal of getting it to the table hot. She fried it and set it aside on a plate with paper towels, and when we finally ate it, it was totally rested at the bone. I don't think that was her conscious intention, but I learned how important that is to a good piece of fried chicken.

Our recipe at Beasley's is informed by what I grew up having. My mom would take chicken, dip it in buttermilk, and then put it into a paper bag and shake it around with some seasoned flour. Brining wasn't something she did, and we certainly didn't have a pressure fryer, so at the restaurant we are connecting tradition with what we've learned. We spent a lot of time figuring out how intense we wanted the brine and seasoning to be. We did rounds of chicken with varying levels of seasoning and varying levels of brine, and when we did the combo of a nice strong brine and zero seasoning—which sounds crazy, but we wanted to know how the pressure frying was affecting it—we found that the pressure frying pulled the salt from the brine into the batter of the chicken, which was a revelation.

When you're making food at a high volume you have the opportunity to limit the variance in seasoning, so you can really nail the consistency. We brine the chicken for twelve hours, dip it in buttermilk, dredge it in flour, then pressure fry it. That seasoning from the meat goes into the breading, and then we hold it in a CVap cabinet, a "controlled vapor" cabinet, which is a high-moisture oven that can run at a very low temperature, like a steam room for the chicken. (And because of the volume at the restaurant, nothing rests in the cabinet very long; most things might be in there for ninety minutes at the longest, and it's such a good holding environment because it doesn't compromise anything.)

We finish the chicken with a three-minute ride in an open fryer, so what you end up with is chicken that is rested at the bone, and when you bite into it all the juice doesn't run out. It has that amazing crispiness on the outside that pairs so well with a drizzle of honey.

The Pressure Fryer

I was reading about how KFC developed the pressure fryer, about how Colonel Harland Sanders decided to throw some oil into a pressure cooker to fry his chicken and then filed for the patent in 1962. It was such a neat piece of technology, and at the same time super terrifying to read about the concept, because you're basically combining two of the more dangerous pieces of equipment in the kitchen. Everyone's scared of a pressure cooker and all the things that can possibly happen—now you're filling it with hot oil. But it is a totally sound and safe piece of equipment and gives us the best chicken-frying scenario.

The Chickens

We work with Springer Mountain Farms in Georgia. We would love to buy local chicken, but we can't find anybody to produce at the volume that we need. If you're buying from a really small producer, all that beautiful, incredible chicken is as expensive as it is because they're often paying up to two dollars per bird to process them properly. Interestingly, and against our will, we sell way more white meat than we do dark meat. And we've figured out that we save a ton of money by just buying whole birds, and no additional breasts, even if we never use the additional stuff. All of our fried-chicken sandwiches are made with thighs, because I think it's so much more flavorful. We also do a saltimbocca dish with thighs at Poole's. We utilize as much extra chicken as we can for stock and other dishes, and the rest we give to our local food bank. We save the money, and we get to do something cool with the extra chicken.

Chicken-Fried Pickles
(aka Chickles)

MAKES 6 TO 8 SNACK SERVINGS

Christensen uses long, thin slices of kosher dills for her fried pickles, but you could use chips, too. She serves them with hot sauce–spiked mayonnaise, but if you get your hands on some good-quality buttermilk, mix it with a spoonful of Dijon mustard and some finely chopped herbs, like parsley, chives, and tarragon, and use that instead.

+ neutral oil, for frying
8 large kosher pickles (about 1 lb), sliced lengthwise into ⅛"-thick strips
2 C buttermilk
3 C all-purpose flour
1 C cornstarch
1 T + 1 t fine sea salt
2 t freshly ground black pepper
+ mayonnaise, preferably Duke's, for serving
+ hot sauce, for serving

1. Add 2 inches of neutral oil to a deep cast-iron skillet or Dutch oven and heat to 350°F.

2. Place the pickle slices in a mixing bowl with the buttermilk and toss to coat. Place the flour, cornstarch, sea salt, and pepper in a bowl, whisk to combine, then transfer dredge to a large brown paper bag. Add the pickle slices to the bag in small batches of 7 or 8, shaking until they're completely coated. Once all of the slices are coated, pull them out of the flour, gently shaking off any excess dredge.

3. Working in batches, place the pickle slices into the skillet of hot oil one by one, giving the slices plenty of room to cook on all sides. Using tongs, continually flip the pickles until the slices are crisp and golden brown, 3–4 minutes total. Transfer the pickles to paper towel–lined plates.

4. Spike the mayonnaise with your favorite hot sauce and serve alongside the freshly fried pickles.

Chicken-Fried Nothing

MAKES 6 TO 8 SERVINGS

These crunchy scraps of batter get fried all on their own. It's like eating fried chicken—without the chicken. "You can also toss them in a fiery Nashville-hot-chicken spice and finish with cool pickles," Christensen says. "Or toss them over a Caesar salad in place of croutons." And if you're in the mood for lunch, pile the bits on a potato roll with a handful of shredded iceberg lettuce and a schmear of mayo.

+ neutral oil, for frying
4 ½ C all-purpose flour
1 ½ C cornstarch
2 T fine sea salt
1 T freshly ground black pepper
2 C buttermilk
+ kosher salt

1. Add 2 inches of neutral oil to a deep cast-iron skillet or Dutch oven and heat to 350°F.

2. Place the flour, cornstarch, sea salt, and pepper in a large mixing bowl, whisk to combine, and level it to create a flat surface. Working in batches, use a tablespoon to distribute spoonfuls of the buttermilk over the surface of the dredge, making an effort to keep them from touching. Let the pools of buttermilk sit on the surface for 60 seconds, and then toss the bowl to allow the excess dredge to coat the buttermilk. Repeat until all buttermilk has been mixed in.

3. Using a sieve, scoop up the dredge-buttermilk mixture and shake off the excess dry dredge. Working in batches, place the dredge-buttermilk flakes into the skillet of hot oil. Using a fryer spoon or spider, stir the crumbs around the oil until they're golden brown and crisp, about 3 minutes, then transfer onto a paper towel–lined plate to drain. Season with salt and serve while hot.

Chicken-Fried Chuck

MAKES 4 SERVINGS

"Our burger joint shares a kitchen with Beasley's, and occasionally they'll do a chicken-fried burger, which is kind of awesome," Christensen says of these deep-fried burger patties, which are coated in a fried-chicken crust, then sandwiched on a roll with the classic fixin's. "They're also super rad served open faced on toasted bread with milk gravy and a sunny-side up egg."

+ neutral oil, for frying
1½ C all-purpose flour
½ C cornstarch
2 t fine sea salt
1 t freshly ground black pepper
1 C buttermilk
4 4-oz burger patties (about ¼" thick)
4 potato rolls
+ iceberg lettuce, sliced tomato, sliced red onion, pickles, mayonnaise, and mustard, for serving

1. Add 2 inches of neutral oil to a deep cast-iron skillet or Dutch oven and heat to 350°F.

2. Place the flour, cornstarch, sea salt, and pepper in a bowl, whisk to combine, then transfer the dredge to a shallow dish. Pour the buttermilk into another shallow dish. Season the chuck patties with salt then dip each patty into the buttermilk, being sure to fully submerge the entire patty. Roll the patty in the dredge, covering all surfaces with the mixture. Repeat with remaining patties.

3. One at a time, carefully lower each patty into the oil.

Using tongs, fry, flipping every 30 seconds, until golden brown and crispy but still pink in the middle, 3–4 minutes total. This will yield a very crispy (but still juicy) burger.

4. Remove the patties from the oil and set on a paper towel–lined plate to rest for 3 minutes. Serve each patty on a roll with lettuce, tomato, red onion, pickles, mayo, and mustard on the side. **LP**

Q: Are We Not Dinosaurs?

A STORY OF DARWIN, EVO-DEVO,
AND THE OUROBOROS OF AVIAN GENEALOGY

BY ARIELLE JOHNSON
ILLUSTRATIONS BY CRISTINA DAURA

As anyone who learned their dino-science from Dr. Alan Grant of *Jurassic Park* knows, birds descended from dinosaurs. And no bird is more closely related on a genetic level to the attractions at Jurassic Park than *Gallus gallus domesticus*, or chickens (and fine, turkeys, too). In fact, today's most populous bird serves not only as our most direct reminder of velociraptors—they also had a part to play in establishing the idea of evolution itself.

While it was the finch that famously spurred Charles Darwin to formulate the theory of evolution, chickens helped him think about selection (natural, artificial, sexual, or otherwise), survival, and fitness, and about how these changes accumulate in organisms over time and generations. Upon returning to England in 1836 with trunkloads of samples from a five-year stint as the onboard gentleman-naturalist of the HMS Beagle during its voyages in and around South America, twenty-seven-year-old Darwin mapped where he'd collected every one of the numerous finches he brought back with him. He noted that while each species had similar bodies, they also had huge differences in beak shape that were unique to their own semi-isolated islands.

Pondering this geographical-morphological relationship—that the species were related to one another, but each adapted to its own specific locality—Darwin began working out ideas on transmutation of one species into another, descent, and adaptation. Because natural history could take him only so far, he looked for inspiration in works on animal breeding and husbandry. In the writings of Sir John Sebright—a politician, agricultural innovator, and breeder of chickens (one of his breeds, the Sebright Bantam, is still around today)—Darwin found some familiar concepts shaping up. In a monograph entitled *The Art of Improving the Breeds of Domestic Animals*, Sebright mused on topics like sexual selection ("The greatest number of females will, of course, fall to the share of the most vigorous males") and the survival of the fittest. He wrote that natural conditions could "select" the traits that get passed onto future generations of animals as much as a farmer deliberately breeding specific animals could.

With visions of chickens selectively coupling in his mind, Darwin developed the foundation of the theory of evolution, though it would take him another twenty years working out the finer points before finally publishing *On the Origin of Species* in 1859. In it, he asked and answered the important question, "If species have descended from other species by insensibly fine gradations, do we not everywhere see innumerable transitional forms?" In other words, why aren't there live specimens or fossils of half-chicken/half-dinosaurs all over the place? And how did we get from giant reptiles to the animals we have today?

He attributed the lack of obvious living transitional forms to the probability that evolved species replaced their original lineages, and hedged that transitional fossils weren't being found because fossils are really hard to make and, in the grand scheme of things, only happen very rarely. "The crust of the earth is a vast museum," he wrote, "but the natural collections have been made only at intervals of time immensely remote." In other words: chill out with the transitional fossil demands.

Then, two years later, a new find gave naturalists a frisson of excitement and vindication.

In a limestone quarry in Bavaria, German scientists excavated a dinosaur-ish fossil that they called the Urvogel ("first bird"), which later became known as the Archaeopteryx ("ancient wing"). It was roughly the size of a raven and had, like most dinosaurs, a long tail, a jaw full of teeth, and a flat sternum. It also had a wishbone, some hollow bones, downy feathers all over its body, and wings covered in asymmetrical flight feathers. It was a clear transitional link between dinosaurs and birds. Darwin's buddy Hugh Falconer, who'd seen the fossil when it was presented at the British Museum in 1863 (Darwin was a recluse, so he stayed home), wrote to Darwin: "Had the Solenhofen quarries been commissioned—by august command—to turn out a strange being à la Darwin—it could not have executed the behest more handsomely—than with the Archaeopteryx."

It took more than a century for the scientific community to come to agreement, but eventually the idea that birds evolved from dinosaurs made its way into high school science classes everywhere. Except Tennessee.

THE UR-CHICKEN,
OR
THANKS AGAIN, DARWIN

It's now widely accepted that the chicken is (mostly) descended directly from a bird called the red jungle fowl, which looks like a bug-eyed, wily cousin of the birds we see on farms, and that has a natural range in South and Southeast Asia, from northern India to Indonesia.

Carolus Linnaeus, the father of modern taxonomy, was perhaps the first Western naturalist to classify the chicken as a relative of the red jungle fowl.

Domestication, in which he fleshed out the argument for the red jungle fowl as the progenitor of the modern chicken.

At the time, colonialism and the Industrial Revolution were combining to create faster and cheaper transport (via the clipper ship) between Britain and its empire. In 1842, a gift of huge Chinese Cochin chickens arrived for the young Queen Victoria, setting off a Tulip Mania-esque frenzy of chicken fancying that burst in the mid-1850s, bringing a lot of exotic chickens and hybrids to England. This gave Darwin access to specimens and data that would not have been available to a similarly educated naturalist of an earlier generation. In addition to extensive comparisons of appearance and analysis of reported data from chicken and jungle-fowl observers in Asia, he also approached the question empirically, through breeding experiments.

He was happy to report that, of the wild jungle-fowl species in Asia, the evidence showed that only red jungle fowl could produce non-sterile offspring with chickens. (A phenomenon that's currently edging the red jungle fowl toward extinction as a distinct species; it interbreeds so much with domestic chickens that it's become tricky to find a red jungle fowl with only wild genetics.) Darwin also bred a purebred black Spanish cock with a harem of hens, most of which were white or black and white, and none of which had shown in their breed lines the characteristic red/orange-shouldered, black-breasted, diagonally plumed tail looks of the red jungle fowl. Despite their achromatic parentage, many of the resulting chicks grew up to have orange and red hackles and shoulders and dark bodies—reverting to ancestral characteristics, according to Darwin.

Rounding out his breeding experiments and ornithological analysis, Darwin drew creatively on scholarship from the humanities as a record of evidence that was no longer tangible. The Greeks called chickens "the Persian birds," but since no chicken-like wild birds had a natural range that included Persia, they probably came to Greece via Persia from somewhere even farther east. In Asian languages, the etymology of words for "chicken" suggested that the word may have originated in Malaysia or Java; and translated ancient Chinese texts suggested chickens were being imported into China in the fifteenth century BCE. Darwin also cited the Bible as evidence, since chickens are mentioned in the New Testament but not in the Old.

Technically, the domestic chicken is classed as a subspecies (Gallus gallus domesticus) of the red jungle fowl (*Gallus gallus*) and a relative of other Gallus species, all of which are different kinds of jungle fowl. But Linnaeus, working a century before Darwin, wasn't advancing an argument about ancestry. ("God created, Linnaeus organized" is one of his famous humblebrags.) To Linnaeus, God had created both the chicken and the jungle fowl, and made them able to breed; thus, they were both Gallus gallus.

The scientific basis for the connection, it turns out, is another of Darwin's great gifts to chickenology.

After publishing *On the Origin of Species* and before writing *The Descent of Man*, Darwin made a deeper exploration into artificial selection in a book called *The Variation of Animals and Plants Under*

After Darwin, the debate over the primary origin of the chicken stalled until the 1990s, with the rapid development of molecular biology and molecular genetics, fields in which precise chemical analysis of DNA and proteins allowed scientists to tell new stories about the relationships between organisms over long stretches of time and across distant places on the globe. Intensive studies of the genetic sequences of modern chickens, ancient chicken bones, and various wild jungle fowl, considered in tandem with archaeological, linguistic, and historical evidence, have enriched, complicated, and sometimes muddied the picture of where and when the jungle fowl became the chicken.

Genetic studies suggest that a key feature of most modern chickens—their yellowish skin—could not have come from red jungle fowl, which have whitish skin, but may have come from gray jungle fowl, a chicken parentage that Darwin had ruled out. Bone analysis from a site in northern China suggests that domesticated chickens were found much farther north (in a climate where no jungle fowl now live) and much earlier (as early as 8,000–5,000 BCE) than anyone expected. Was this the product of an earlier original domestication event, outside the current range of the red jungle fowl that subsequently spread southward? Or was the chicken domesticated multiple times in parallel? (Or, as

has been suggested in critical follow-ups, mitochondrial DNA confirmation aside, could the bones have been misidentified? It's happened, more than once, before.) As of now, the jury is still out.

BETTER LIVING THROUGH ARTIFICIAL SELECTION AND CHEMISTRY

In the nineteenth and early twentieth centuries, interest arose in "improving" breeds to make them grow larger, faster, more efficiently, or lay more eggs. Rearing flocks specifically for egg laying became common (with the male chicks in these flocks used as "broilers," or meat chickens), especially after World War I.

Over successive generations of selective breeding—really accelerating after World War II—chickens have been transformed from a variety of breeds that gave both eggs and meat into an industrial bioreactor for turning corn into protein as efficiently as possible. With these chickens, you can choose eggs or meat, not both. And you certainly don't get to choose flavor.

The infamous Chicken of Tomorrow contest of 1948 marked a watershed moment in the creation of the industrial breeds that make up most of the chickens alive today. It started innocently enough—with beef being rationed during the war, Americans' chicken consumption almost

Darwin himself didn't know exactly what the mechanism for evolution was. He certainly didn't know about genes, with genetics not really established as a science until the early days of the twentieth century; or DNA, which wasn't understood to be the storage molecule for genetic information until the 1940s. Now we know that evolution is driven by random mutation at the molecular level of DNA—if the mutation hurts the organism's fitness or sexual attractiveness (which is what usually happens), that organism doesn't reproduce, doesn't pass the mutation on to its children, and the mutation dies out. If the mutation helps the organism adapt to its environment or makes it sexier to prospective mates, then the mutation is passed on. A lot of the differences in purebred heirloom chickens come from random mutations that humans decided to propagate. When heirlooms are bred together, the new hybrid gets genes from its parents, each one with different alterations to the original red jungle fowl like-genome.

doubled, and grocers were interested in keeping sales up. A&P launched a promotion for chicken breeders of all stripes to submit for consideration the largest, most breasty, picture-perfect bird that could be raised in twelve weeks on the least possible food. The winning chickens were a hybrid, the first generation of a cross between a New Hampshire hen and a California Cornish rooster. At twelve weeks, they weighed 3.75 pounds each; an improvement on the contemporary average of three pounds.

Selective breeding continued over subsequent years, expanding from grocery chains to universities' animal-science departments and commercial chicken breeders. By 1973, chickens were reaching maturity at eight and a half weeks. It's now possible to rear chicks that reach maturity even faster, in five weeks, and put on four pounds and change in that time.

A few other developments helped make this possible. The 1950s and '60s were the first decades of the heyday of cheap corn, thanks to intensive farming methods, commercial seed lines, and selective breeding. Previously, "free-range" chickens weren't a thing, because all chickens were free to range outside and eat grasses, insects, and grubs, even if they were fed largely grain-based chicken feed. Chicken farmers actually had to let their animals forage—if they didn't, they got metabolic diseases (similar to beriberi and anemia in humans) from missing the micronutrients they would usually get from their grub supplements.

This brings us to the third element of

Perfect Chicken but Tasteless

the commercial-chicken trifecta: the "vital essences," or vitamins and minerals, discovered in the early part of the twentieth century. With these isolated micronutrients in hand, chicken farmers could fortify inexpensive corn and create a feed that fattened chickens quickly without killing them. This allowed producers to go from flocks of fifty to two hundred chickens to facilities with thousands upon thousands of chickens, since there was no longer any need to let chickens out onto pasture to keep them alive.

And just like that, you've got a recipe for billions of giant, inexpensive, tasteless chickens.

CHICKENS OF FUTURE PAST

Back to chicken's dino roots. We know that toward the end of the Jurassic period, a branch of ancestrally carnivorous theropods emerged as ancient birds. Recent fossil finds, like the sinosauropteryx (discovered in 1996 in Liaoning Province in China, and covered in primitive downy

feathers), quill knobs found on velociraptors, and wing and tail segments encased in amber, show that non-avian theropod dinosaurs (cousins to ancient birds, though not actually birds) commonly had feathers, suggesting that feathers evolved before birds did.

And while we haven't been able to isolate dinosaur DNA yet (sorry, Jurassic Park fans), we've learned a lot about which genetic changes are necessary to make changes in an animal's shape. The basic map of a vertebrate isn't revised wholesale when something like a bird emerges from the lineage of dinosaurs. Dinosaurs and chickens (and humans) have skulls with two eyes, a rib cage, a pelvis, a spine, and forelimbs and hind limbs. Dinosaurs had tails where chickens have a stumpy structure called a pygostyle, jaws and teeth where chickens have beaks, and their five-fingered front limbs differ from chickens' three-appendaged wings (though those wings develop in the chicken embryo from hand-like structures).

We've learned from a new branch of science called evolutionary developmental

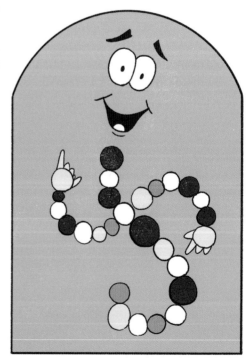

biology (or evo-devo) that the evolved changes in the anatomy of an adult organism are generally laid out as it develops from a single-celled zygote through its embryonic phase into a baby animal. This development isn't directly guided by a gene that codes for a tail or a beak, per se, but (because nothing in nature is ever simple) from feedback among the so-called Hox genes, other genes that produce enzymes that start and stop growth, and genes that directly cause different types of cells to grow. The Hox genes are the master guides of the development of an embryo along its head-to-tail axis: change one Hox gene in a fruit fly, and it will develop wings where its antennae should be; change another, and it will grow an extra pair of wings. The Hox genes evolved very early in the evolutionary tree—about 500 million years ago, and are found with extremely similar sequences throughout the animal kingdom (fruit flies, chickens, and humans alike).

But crucially, the Hox genes don't code for legs or wings—the proteins they code for bind to other sections of DNA, and by binding, turn those genes off and on. The genes that Hox proteins bind to don't code for a leg or a wing either; they code for proteins that control other genes, the coordination of which eventually leads to bone or eye (or wing or tail) development. Hox genes, and the genes that Hox proteins bind to, are called transcription factors: they control which sections of DNA get read and transcribed into RNA, which then gets translated by the ribosome into a protein. An organism can easily have dozens of transcription factor genes, each of which can bind to and regulate a hundred or more target genes. And the target genes might code for a specific enzyme or type of tissue, but just as often they are also regulatory genes, so what gets switched on or off is yet another cascade of switching.

IF IT SOUNDS COMPLICATED, IT IS.

But the basic takeaway is that the big physical differences in, say, a bird and a dinosaur don't actually come from changes in the genes that directly build the tail or wing, but in genetic changes that affect the regulation of those genes. Which means that the changes in dinosaurs that led, eventually, to the chicken, were regulatory: down regulation of tail development, changes in forelimb development that mutated hands into wings, changes in the genes that direct the locations where feather follicles develop, and inactivation (but not necessarily deletion) of genes that cause tooth buds to develop, among others.

Most of you will take this as food for thought or a factoid for your next dinner party, or maybe an opportunity to get philosophical with yourself. (All human beauty comes from arbitrary differences in the regulation of cells that make structural materials, and the face that gives me my social currency is just an emergent property of transcription factors making slight differences in bone secretion rates in cells in different locations! My idea of myself is an illusion! Society is a sham!) A paleontologist named Jack Horner is taking it and running with it—backward in time. He looked at evo-devo and decided that if we know how gene regulation changed tooth into beak formation in the chicken

embryo, then we can just as easily regulate in the other direction, creating "experimental atavisms," causing a chicken embryo that has the code for a beak to develop teeth. We can stimulate the embryonic chicken's pygostyle to develop into a tail; swoop in and downregulate the growth of the long digits that make up the wing, thus creating a hand instead; and alter the regulation pathway that directs where feathers develop.

You'd think that as the science advisor for Jurassic Park (he was, seriously, and also was the inspiration for Dr. Alan Grant), Horner would know better than to mess with nature like this. "Life finds a way," after all, and rarely are the results clean or predictable, but he's forging ahead, working with evo-devo labs that study the pertinent regulatory networks in embryos. When and if they create an embryo that can actually grow (remember the scene in Alien: Resurrection when Ripley finds all the horribly mutated earlier attempts at cloning her? That's basically what an evo-devo lab's archive looks like, with chicken), it remains to be seen whether their ethics oversight committee will let them hatch it. But as a common, genetically understood bird, chickens are the standard avian model organism, and thus the natural subject of Horner's reverse evolution. What came from dinosaurs through jungle fowl, and Darwin's research into the modern chicken, may loop the evolutionary tree into a circle, taking us to dinosaurs once more. LP

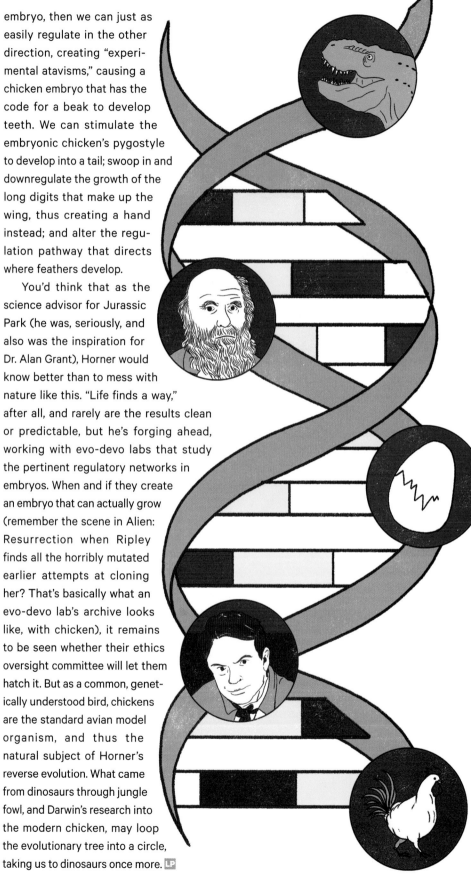

Matt Furie

When the Slowing Gets Big, the Big Start Slowing:

The Change Coming to Chicken

By Chris Nuttall-Smith

Photographs by Molly Matalon

I SPENT WEEKS

trying to get an audience with Dr. Paul Aho, but the great man never returned my calls or e-mails. Aho is Big Chicken's number-one egghead, an international poultry economist who works from a tidy, two-story, tree-shrouded house near Hartford, Connecticut (thanks, Google Street View!).

For the past thirty years, his columns in trade journals like *Broiler Industry* were required reading—a celebration of maximalist American innovation applied to one of the most efficient (if increasingly insipid) industrial animal proteins on earth.

He marveled as genetic advancements and fine-tuned feeding turned broiler chickens—that's the insider term for meat birds—into chest-heavy, weak-kneed, fast-growing freaks of modern breeding. Broilers ballooned from an average size at slaughter of just more than four pounds in the early 1980s to more than ten pounds at the upper end today. (Chicken breasts can now weigh more than entire chickens did in the 1950s.) And the best part, to Aho, was how cheaply we could do it. Ingenuity and economy reduced the cost of producing a pound of chicken by half. Those jumbo-sized chicken breasts, for instance, were transformed in thirty years from "a luxury product sold in small quantities to the wealthy," into the cut-rate makings of McNuggets. In one particularly triumphalist dispatch, Aho wrote that the chicken had at long last become America's "king of meats."

Aho made a comparison a couple of years ago that struck me. In its constant quest to find efficiency in technology, the broiler industry, he wrote, was a lot like the tech industry. His analogy helped me see the modern chicken in a whole new way. Those birds—the Cobb 500, the Ross 708, the Arbor Acres Plus, to cite just a few of the most popular current models—were not

mere animals. They were the avian kingdom's answers to the Microsoft Surface Book and the HP Z240 Workstation: all supercharged bloatware and hair-trigger health problems, but damned if you couldn't churn them out ever more quickly and make truckloads of money along the way.

I wanted to ask Aho about all this, and especially about how that relentless progress seems primed these days to be flipped on its cockscombed head. Because after decades of bigger-and-faster-is-better breeding, the hottest new thing in America's broiler industry is a smaller, less efficient chicken that eats more feed and takes longer to grow. It's Pong in the age of Pokémon Go, and yet some of America's biggest food and agriculture giants are lining up to lock in their supply.

THE BREWING STORM

While the health issues common to high-performance chickens have long been known, a paper published in the January 2012 issue of the scientific journal *Nutrients* documented an alarming and potentially more costly class of problems. The paper's topic was the known diseases, disfigurations, "degenerative myopathies," and otherwise unappetizing misfortunes

that can befall the modern chicken's flesh before it hits the table—problems the chicken-eating public had started to see. I'm not sure if I'd rather find "green muscle disease" or "pale, soft, exudative" tissue in my plastic-wrapped family pack of boneless, skinless chicken breasts. And absent a taste test I hope to never conduct, it's a toss-up whether either of those is preferable to "white striping" and "woody breast," which one poultry executive recently described to the *Wall Street Journal* as feeling like "my thigh when I get a cramp playing tennis, there's a knot in the meat." His description was apt: the woody breast pictures I've seen do look like old white man thighs, if that old white man had advanced jaundice and a particularly revolting case of varicose veins. It's not just the look: woody breast reportedly imparts a gummy chew.

The incidence of these issues has spiked in the past few years. White striping and woody breast, mostly unknown even within the industry until around 2011, can now appear in broiler flocks at rates of up to 79 percent and 10 percent, respectively. Green muscle disease has started turning up even on small free-range farms. The cause, according to the authors of the *Nutrients* paper, is the ever-faster-growing chickens. Or as they put it: "It is believed that genetic progress has put more stress on the growing bird and it has resulted in histological and biochemical modifications of the muscle tissue by impairing some meat-quality traits."

What all this means is that the mantra of "heavier, quicker, cheaper" is no longer just an animal-welfare problem, but also an economic one. Unlike the gastrointestinal diseases, rampant lethargy, and lameness that are everyday annoyances in the fast-growth broiler racket—or the heart attacks that occur in appalling numbers—meat-quality issues are harder to accept as a cost of doing business. While few people outside the industry can picture what a 4.8 percent average mortality rate looks like, gummy, mushy, green-tinged, white-striped, and blood-spotted meat is easy to spot, and reject.

This all matters because it underscores the debate that's building inside the chicken business. The slow-growing broiler camp has bet that the only way to fix the industry is to change the model altogether. "At the end of the day the genetics of the bird are limiting," said Anne Malleau, executive director of Global Animal Partnership (GAP), an influential animal-welfare group that's campaigning, along with the Humane Society of the United States, for slower-growth broilers. "We've pushed it a little bit over the edge."

A FIRST ATTEMPT

David Pitman saw that edge while on a trip to Europe in 2008. His family had been growing poultry in California's San Joaquin Valley for more than fifty years. But Pitman had come to have misgivings about the kinds of birds his family raised. Their flocks, mostly Cobb 500s, grew fat fast, and cheap, but too many were sickly and listless. Because they grew so big in so little time on undeveloped legs, even walking was too much for some of the birds.

In England and France, he saw a different sort of chicken business. England's broiler industry, under pressure from animal-welfare groups, had started moving toward chickens that grew more slowly—they took fifty-six and seventy days to get to market size, instead of fast-growing broilers' forty-two or fewer. In France, slow-growing birds had long been prized for their flavor and texture, with some varieties, like the famed Poulet de Bresse, considered national culinary treasures. (The Netherlands, too, soon got in on the action; within a few years of Pitman's first European visit, the country

began to raise slow-growers at scale, at a profit, in numbers to fill the meat cases at suburban hypermarts.

As soon as he landed back in California, Pitman took his plans to his dad, the patriarch of the family business. "My dad said, 'Whoa, whoa, whoa, we still gotta make bank payments. Let's go through this.'" David's father let him test his plans on a single farm with room for ten thousand birds per week.

Pitman got the chicks from France and starting raising them. What those birds lost in speed-to-slaughter they gained in

SHOT AT PITMAN FAMILY FARMS IN ORANGE COVE, CA

ease of raising. The lameness and listlessness all but disappeared. Better still, they didn't drop dead, he said, from the sorts of diseases more appropriate to palliative-care units than chicken barns.

But while raising them was a pleasure, marketing them was not. This was 2009 still, and almost nobody in America had heard of slow-growing chickens, much less tasted one. In America, chicken then (as now, for the most part) was *chicken*. You could get organic chicken, air-chilled chicken, grain-fed chicken, free-range chicken, and kosher and halal chicken, certainly, but nobody troubled ordinary customers with age-to-slaughter or breed details. "I was preaching something that no one was ready to know about," Pitman said. After a few years, he packed his experiment in.

A few months after he'd sent his last slow-growing flock to slaughter, Pitman got a call from one of the meat buyers at Whole Foods who told him slow-growing chickens were going to be the next big thing. He asked, "Can we get some next week?'"

A STEP BACK IN TIME, AND A STEP FORWARD

Blake Evans's grandfather helped usher in the bigger-faster-cheaper movement in the 1950s. An amateur geneticist, he was an inductee to the American Poultry Historical Society's Hall of Fame. The rooster he developed, called the Peterson Male, remains among the more important broiler genetic lines in America. Evans sold it all a few years back: the family's $160 million per year commodity broiler business went to one of the poultry giants, while the rights to the Peterson Male went to Aviagen, the world's second-biggest breeding firm.

With that sale completed, Evans turned back in time. "We decided that we needed to reach back to some heritage genetics and work towards building a bird more or less from the ground up," he said. "What I'm doing now is trying to fix what was done years ago."

Evans started raising his new line in 2013 at his farm in Decatur, Arkansas. He was happy enough with the results to give the white-feathered, bare-necked cross a name: the Crystal Lake Free Ranger.

He laughed when I asked how his birds are different from the commodity ones sired by his grandfather's rooster. He noted the same things Pitman had—that they walked with ease and perched up high, and foraged and dust-bathed like real chickens. And when he opens the barn doors to let them outside, his slow-growers line up "like third graders at recess. You can tell that the genetics brought this to the bird. It's kind of like you brought back its natural characteristics or instincts... It's almost like they're athletes instead of couch potatoes."

AT THE HATCHERY

Sean Holcombe works for Hubbard, one of the three global genetics companies (Aviagen and Cobb-Vantress are the others) that control the broiler breeder trade: they develop the genetic lines and hatch the birds that broiler growers raise.

Until three years ago, Hubbard didn't bother keeping grandparent slow-growth breeder flocks in its North American farms. The trade was small enough that when an order came in, they'd just ship in the eggs from France.

These days, Hubbard keeps two separate slow-growing female lines and six male lines here. Hubbard's U.S. slow-grower sales were up 40 percent in 2015, said Holcombe—slow-growth is the company's fastest-growing market. And that's before you factor in what happened last March, when the Global Animal Partnership announced it was making slow-growing broilers its next crusade. "The way I look at it, it's kind of like cage free," said Anne Malleau. "It's going to happen."

Whole Foods signed on immediately; the retailer plans to eliminate fast-growing breeds from its stores entirely by 2024. (This is not entirely surprising: Whole Foods founded the Global Animal Partnership, and the two organizations share key staff, including Malleau. GAP advocates for animal welfare on the farm and at slaughterhouses, and certifies farms and food companies that adopt its standards.)

A few months later, Perdue Farms, which produces 13 million chickens weekly (it's the fourth-largest broiler business in the U.S.), said it was exploring slower-growth genetics as part of its own animal-welfare plan, which will also improve living conditions and make its slaughterhouses more humane. (Perdue, to its credit, is also the only top broiler producer to entirely remove antibiotics from its operations.) The company has a test barn up and running already, said company executive Dr. Bruce Stewart-Brown.

This past fall, the U.S. divisions of Compass Group and Aramark, the world's two largest food-service companies, also jumped in, announcing that they, too, would begin sourcing only slow-growing

chickens, and plan to accomplish this in the next eight years. A few weeks later, competitors Sodexo USA, Delaware North, and Centerplate made the same move.

At Hubbard, in Tennessee, Sean Holcombe's phone has started ringing in a way he isn't used to. "I've had calls from Panera and McDonald's and on and on and on, different people calling and trying to get more and more information as to what this is going to look like," he told me. (Panera has since announced it's moving to slower-growth birds.)

That sort of snowball effect is exactly the reaction a lot of people in the food industry expected—they've seen this sort of shift already with the campaigns to get rid of gestation crates for pigs and routine antibiotic use in broiler houses, and with the widespread adoption, in just the past couple of years, of cage-free eggs.

IS THE SKY FALLING?

There is an environmental cost to switching over to birds that eat more food and give less meat. Diana Prichard, a small-scale hog farmer in Michigan who blogs about her business at *Righteous Bacon*, estimated the additional 11 million bushels of feed needed just for the first wave of slow-growth commitments—Whole Foods and a

few GAP-accredited farms—would require the fruits of 112,000 acres of cropland, or more than half the area of New York City. "Which means Whole Foods' feel-good poultry campaign either requires us to take more than 112,000 acres out of wildlife habitat and put it into cropland," Prichard wrote, "or all of that additional demand will fall on current cropland, causing a run up in grain—and by extension food—prices."

That issue—more feed for less meat is harder on the planet—will force consumers to decide how much they value welfare. "You're gonna need more chicken houses, more chickens, and more feed and more water to produce the same pounds of meat that you are today," said Hubbard's Sean Holcombe. He added, "That is going to happen. But the other way of looking at it is, there's a portion of our consumers, especially very young, very far removed from the farm, that is going to quit buying products that are not what they feel are raised in a humane manner. So maybe the model we have isn't sustainable long-term if the consumer is going to back away."

And the sector's got a few other hurdles to overcome. Price, for instance. At Whole Foods, the retailer's fifty-six-day chicken sells for $4 to $6 per pound, a 60 percent premium on its regular (which is to say: antibiotic-free, GMO-free) birds. Many in the business say that the price difference should fall as producers find efficiencies in how they raise, process, and feed the birds (a slow-grower benefit: they don't need nearly such high-performance feed as their fast-growing cousins). Slow-growth genetics, a relative backwater until recently, have room yet for more efficiency, and as the market for slow-growth chicken expands, economies of scale could also help.

Eating preferences will have an impact on slow growth's popularity, too: every time

somebody chooses white meat instead of dark, it makes the economics tougher to reconcile. Modern, fast-growing chickens have been bred to be chesty because that's where the money is: a Cobb 700 grown to maximum weight finishes out at nearly 30 percent boneless breast. Slow-growers, by comparison, top out at around 20 percent white meat, so it's harder to recoup the cost of farming them at retail. "If all anybody wants is just the breast meat from a slow-growing bird, wow, that's going to carry a lot of economics," said Stewart-Brown.

And there are plenty of people within the industry who argue that it makes more sense to fix the problems associated with fast-growing broilers than to throw them out altogether. Dr. Stephen Collett, a clinical professor at the University of Georgia's Poultry Diagnostic and Research Center, says the rampant gut issues, for instance, that are caused by the birds' hardwired overeating can be fixed with smarter feeding programs; in one experiment, poultry researchers have begun fitting birds with transponders that monitor their intake and slowly dole out feed. All these fixes require is the will and the resources, said Collett. "My experience with the U.S. is that the market is much more tentative and

slower to move, but when it does move, it moves with tremendous speed."

Dr. Bill Muir, a poultry geneticist with Purdue University's Center for Animal Welfare Science, agrees that the industry's efforts should focus first on fixing what it's got. Leg health, he said, could be fixed within a few generations through simple breeding. (A downside: it would dilute the breeders' ability to breed for speed and size.) In human terms, said Muir, that fix is possible within four to ten years.

Yet all that possibility is undermined by another, far more powerful reality. Big Chicken doesn't take kindly to being told how it should operate. The movement to antibiotic-free farming, to cite just one recent example, was greeted with Chicken Little–style histrionics even as major broiler growers like Perdue had already proved it both possible and profitable. (Money line from the number-three U.S. broiler company, Sanderson Farms: "More animals will suffer and/or die for no one's benefit.")

As for slow growth, the broiler industry's biggest lobby group has so far gone full-out passive-aggressive to ward away change. When Compass Group and Aramark announced their new purchasing plans, the National Chicken Council claimed that moving to slow-growing broilers would "have a devastating effect on the environment."

"We're committed to continual improvement, but those improvements should be dictated by science and data, not animal-rights activists or emotional rhetoric that is unsupported by facts," their statement read.

The fact is that the industry has had years to address the needs for "continual improvement"—for example, to fix its flagship product's inability to walk. And now it's crying foul even as it needs to correct that, plus the woody breast, the white striping, the green muscle disease, the drop-dead heart attacks, the dependence on antibiotics, *and* the susceptibility to gut diseases.

Dr. Margaret Derry, a historian of animal breeding, raised one other issue with the move to slow-growers: it's uncivilized, more or less. "To say that the idea is to produce animals that take longer to finish and produce less meat and use more feed, I have never heard of that happening before. And I am a historian who knows a fair amount about animal breeding in Northern Europe and North America in the last four hundred years."

TASTES LIKE CHICKEN

Maybe it comes down to taste. It is gospel in the food-writing business that the consumption of any bird that's slow-growing, heritage-bred, pasture-raised, and/or Montessori-educated is, by convention, to be treated as a life-affirming accomplishment, and the eating of regular chicken is as depressing as an art film about childhood leukemia set in the dish pit of a Las Vegas Applebee's directed by Lars von Trier. Michael Pollan, describing a dinner of pasture-raised chicken in *The Omnivore's Dilemma,* wrote, "The skin had turned the color of mahogany and the texture of parchment, almost like a Peking duck, and the meat itself was moist, dense, and almost shockingly flavorful… which is to say, I suppose, that it chimed with that capitalized idea of Chicken we hold in our heads but seldom taste anymore."

Mark Schatzker, who (brilliantly) wrote about slow-growing chicken in his book *The Dorito Effect,* calls his chapter on commodity chicken "Big Bland." Of his experience eating a heritage bird, he says, "This was get-up-out-of-your-chair-and-start-dancing fried chicken. It brought on a state of giddiness that verged on the evangelical. You know chicken is good when you want to run down the street telling strangers about it."

Which, I don't know, maybe I'm eating chicken wrong. While it doesn't typically move me to dancing, I can happily down half of a properly seasoned and roasted grocery store chicken in a single, sigh-punctuated go. The promise of slower-growing chicken, though, isn't just that it's better for the birds (which it is), or that they don't get woody breast and green muscle disease (which they don't), or that they're easier to raise without antibiotics (which they typically are). It's that the chicken won't just taste like *chicken*.

Stewart-Brown of Perdue Farms, a company that was built on producing and processing commodity chicken in unimaginable volumes, said, "If there's an opportunity for better taste and eating experience, we'd like to find that," which is not the sort of thing that vice presidents at vertically integrated, $6.3 billion a year chicken companies usually go around and say. When I mentioned how strange it was, he agreed. "I'm going to say it's unusual," adding, "this is not generic chicken."

Theo Weening, Whole Foods's global meat coordinator, said of his first experience with David Pitman's chicken, "It had flavor without adding marinades or a lot of seasonings. It was completely different."

There's a fair bit of research backing that up: the older the bird, the bigger the taste. In one of my favorite flavor studies of all time, a pair of French researchers charted chicken flavor, tenderness, and juiciness against days to slaughter and testicular weight. (Pro tip: always buy the chicken with the biggest nads.)

But even some slow-growth proponents admit that the flavor differences between a forty-two-day bird and a fifty-six-day one aren't always that pronounced—in research that Hubbard has done in the U.S., tasters noted differences only about half the time.

How a bird tastes can depend just as much on the breed of chicken, what it ate, how it was raised, and how it was slaughtered. That can really change when you get up above sixty days, when the taste starts to stand out.

Early this winter I drove to a small-scale organic farm that raises slow-growers.

The fields were covered in dirty snow, and the last of the flock had been frozen solid for the past couple months. "You wanted a five-pounder, right?" the farmer asked. It had been raised on pasture, he said, and he'd sent it to slaughter at sixty-three days.

Thawed but uncooked, it looked for all the world like a supermarket job. But after it had been seasoned, roasted crisply golden, and rested a few minutes—after I sliced into the breast and thigh and the juices started running and the smell of it filled my kitchen, the similarities fell away. The color of the leg and thigh meat was darker and the texture denser. The breast meat felt firmer and looked more creamy beige than Styrofoam white. All I could think as I breathed in the steam was that it was somehow richer and more chickeny, in the same way dry-aged beef tastes more strongly of beef. (No, I did not start dancing.) As for the taste, it *wasn't* your usual chicken. It was delicious enough that the animal-welfare benefits felt almost beside the point.

No matter why people eat it, slow-growth chicken is coming. As the likes of Compass Group and Whole Foods step up and demand slow-growth chickens, broiler breeders and growers step in to fill demand. David Pitman, out in California, sees that eight years after he first decided slower growers are the future, the rest of the industry has started catching up. He said, "I think this is going to explode." **LP**

Fried Chicken
of the
World

P oultry gets crisped in sizzling oil all over the world in traditions that succeed and exist independently of American fried chicken. The wild success of KFC has increased fried chicken's popularity abroad but, in satisfying circularity, it has also led to American outposts of Guatemalan and Korean fried chicken joints that have changed the way Americans eat and think about the dish. Come with us on a breezy little tour of the fried chickens of the world.

By Emily Johnson   *Photographs by Pete Deevakul*

Singapore
Har Cheong Gai

Har cheong gai, or prawn-paste chicken, is the signature Singaporean style of fried chicken, found in hawker centers or as a specialty of *zi char* stalls serving home-style Chinese food.

The prawn paste preferred in Singapore is gray, thick, gloopy, and extremely fragrant before it is cooked. It's thinned into a marinade with Shaoxing wine, ginger, soy sauce, sugar, and sometimes a little oyster sauce and MSG. The chicken then sits overnight in a batter made with the marinade, flour, and potato starch before being fried the next day.

"It is best eaten by itself, as there is so much umami flavor from the shrimp paste, but it's usually served with a chili sauce," says Singaporean-born chef Nicholas Tang, of DBGB in New York. "The best har cheong gai I've ever eaten is at this steamboat place called Whampoa Keng Fish Head. We compete with my dad over who can best eat the chicken, but my dad always wins. He loves it—he always eats right down to the bone."

Indonesia
Ayam Goreng

Robyn Eckhardt writes about food and travel in Asia and Turkey.

How many ways can you fry a chicken? In Indonesia, a country whose inhabitants are spread across some ten thousand islands (of a total of over seventeen thousand), the methods are myriad. But the city of Yogyakarta's deluxe version of fried chicken—a twice-cooked bird that's served mounded with spiced crispy bits—claims particularly widespread appeal. Eaten from early morning until late at night, the dish is typically part of a meal that includes white rice, *lalapan* (raw vegetables like sliced cucumbers and tomatoes), and a fiery *sambal trassi* (shrimp paste), palm sugar, and chilies pounded together.

Making *ayam goreng yogya*, as the dish is known beyond its hometown, requires commitment. First, there's the *bumbu* (spice paste), a ground mixture of shallots, garlic, ginger, lemongrass, salt, coriander seeds, and perhaps candlenuts. Along with dark palm sugar and *daun salam* (often described as Indonesian bay leaf, though it is not a member of the laurel family), the bumbu is mixed with coconut (or regular) water to make a poaching liquid for the chicken. After the chicken is removed, the poaching liquid is strained to remove sediment and mixed with starch to form a pourable batter. The bird is fried and then so is the batter, in the same oil. Eaten together, the two components—tender, moist, spice-imbued chicken and crunchy spice crackles—are an extravaganza of texture, seasoning and, well, grease.

Ayam goreng yogya is said to have been invented several decades ago by one Mbok Berek, who may have been inspired by a similar version of fried chicken associated with Kalasan, a village outside the city. She began selling it from a roadside *warung* and then expanded to a namesake chain of ayam goreng shops. Today the dish is the main menu item at Ayam Goreng Suharti, a small fried chicken chain founded by Mbok Berek's granddaughter. In its hometown, it remains ubiquitous.

—*Robyn Eckhardt*

Vietnam
Ga Chien

Calvin Godfrey is a writer and photographer based in Ho Chi Minh City.

In Vietnam, fried chicken gets slathered in a caramel made with *nuoc mam*—fish sauce, the lifeblood of the nation. The fish-sauce glaze for the chicken wings is called *mam kho quet* (braised "wicking" sauce) and can be eaten with fresh or steamed vegetables, but it takes on an otherworldliness when applied to chicken, particularly wings.

The first time I encountered the dish was at the very end of my first year in Vietnam. I planned to go home and forget about the country when my girlfriend invited me to dinner at her mom's house. Her mother, originally from the northern city of Nam Dinh, had prepared her signature sticky rice and fish-sauce-glazed chicken wings.

The meal hooked me. I couldn't speak any Vietnamese then, so I just smiled and ate lots of wings. I later moved in to that house, and those wings became a major part of my life, as did the family. I've looked for a commercial place that does an equally excellent version of the dish and have never really found it.

Naturally, however, there's more than one way to fry a chicken in Vietnam. Sometimes chicken is scored and briefly marinated in fish sauce and shallots and given a sprinkle of *bot nem* (a powder of spices, salt, and MSG) before it is fried; this is not a bad thing. This style often appears on the menu at *quan nhau* places (sidewalk drinking spots), but it's usually subpar. There's a highly overrated restaurant in Ho Chi Minh City called Com Ga Xoi Mo Su Su, where a man has jury-rigged a fat fryer into a grease waterfall, in which he fries chicken. In my opinion, none of these offerings hold a candle to a plate of *canh ga chien nuoc mam* and sticky rice eaten at home.

—*Calvin Godfrey*

Thailand
Gai Tod

Andy Ricker is the chef and owner of the Pok Pok restaurants in Portland, New York, and LA.

Fried chicken is not a complicated or fancy dish in Thailand. It's something you find on the streets everywhere.

Every city has a fried chicken specialist, and there are as many ways to fry chicken as there are vendors. But there are several common iterations. *Gai tod hat yai* is a deep-fried chicken from the south made with a red, spicy batter that contains either red chili or red curry paste. *Gai tod kamin*—chicken fried with turmeric—is another style of southern fried chicken. It's typically marinated in MSG, turmeric, and other seasonings. They fry the chicken with lots of shallots and garlic and serve the chicken piled high with the crisp-fried aromatics. There are also people who don't do anything to the chicken. No batter, dredge, nothing—they might cut and dry it for a while first, and then it goes straight into the oil. There's a guy in Nan Province who takes a whole chicken, rubs it with salt and *makhwaen,* a type of prickly ash, and then fries the whole bird.

Unless you're in a fast-food restaurant (KFC is the most popular one in the country), almost all fried chicken is cooked in palm oil in a large, thick-bottomed aluminum or steel wok at around 300 degrees.

My favorite place for fried chicken is Midnight Fried Chicken (ไก่ทอดเที่ยงคืน) in Chiang Mai. It's where you go after the bars and nightclubs close—it opens at about 10:30 p.m. and stays open until 4:30 a.m. They fry more than just chicken—they do pork belly, fish, intestines—but the chicken is what they're known for. There's a super crispy crust that they accomplish with a very thin batter, and they fry the hell out of the chicken in this super-black oil. The secret to the batter is the use of *nam poon sai,* or slaked-lime water. It's used often in batters in Thai cooking because the added alkalinity makes stuff really crispy.

I like to order chicken *nam prik* there, which means it comes with various chili pastes: *nam prik ta-dang,* which is a very hot chili paste, and *nam prik noom,* which is a green chili paste. Typically I'll get some pieces of fried chicken, one of the nam prik, some boiled eggs, maybe some deep-fried dried pork or beef, and some sticky rice.

When you roll up there, be warned: they're not friendly or hospitable. A few years back, when a customer gave the owner shit for not opening early enough, he went in the back, grabbed a gun, and shot the guy. He went to jail, but now everybody knows not to mess with the counter guys ever again.

—Andy Ricker

India
Kerala Fried Chicken

Asha Gomez is the chef of Spice to Table in Atlanta.

I grew up eating fried chicken in Kerala, which is a region at the southernmost tip of India, kind of nestled between the Arabian Sea and the Indian Ocean. In South India, we actually do a lot of meat-forward dishes, so you'll tend to see fried chicken there more than other areas, especially in the north of India, where the vast majority of people are vegetarians due to religious affiliation. I was raised Roman Catholic, so we'd go to mass and then come back home and eat fried chicken for lunch or dinner, just like in the American South.

There are two variations of fried chicken I love eating in Kerala. My mom's is similar to fried chicken in the American South in that it's marinated, dredged in flour, and deep-fried. My mom would blend together buttermilk, ginger, garlic, cilantro, mint, and green chili, and then marinate the chicken for twenty-four hours. Once it came out, she'd dredge it in flour and a garam-masala spice blend. In my mother's kitchen, we'd deep-fry it in coconut oil, but in the States, I fry in vegetable oil and drizzle coconut oil over the top, because coconut oil is expensive here. In the coastal areas, every household makes this kind of chicken.

There's another dish that's called *kozhi porichathu,* which is served at *thattukada,* or roadside stands. The roadside guys open their shops past ten p.m., so it's strictly for truck drivers. The chicken is marinated with chilies and whole cloves of garlic that are crushed up with the skin on. There's no flour involved. It's then deep-fried in coconut oil with ginger and the garlic, and served topped with all of the aromatics. It's served on top of *malabar parotta,* which is a type of bread from the region. They wrap it up in a banana leaf and newspaper and give it to you. Whenever I return to my motherland, my family knows to come to the airport with a package of it. My youth comes flooding back to me; I'm right back in the tenth grade, sneaking out to eat this chicken with my friends.

—Asha Gomez

India

Chicken Manchurian

Garlic chicken, chili chicken, chicken 65, and chicken lollipops all fall under the category of Indian-Chinese cuisine that originated in Calcutta during the eighteenth century. Indo-Chinese cuisine would eventually make its way to Mumbai, where a chef would invent chicken Manchurian.

Cubes of chicken are coated in cornstarch and egg, deep-fried, then tossed in a sauce made with onions, chilies, garlic, soy sauce, and vinegar. The dish has spawned any number of spin-off fried chicken dishes in the same family line; sometimes the sauce contains ketchup, sometimes MSG. Many of the dishes contain Indian flavors in the form of garam masala and hearty garnishes of fresh cilantro leaves.

One popular iteration is the chicken lollipop, where the meat is frenched from the bone of either a wing or a drumette, marinated in garlic paste, chili paste, soy sauce, vinegar, and occasionally spices such as cumin, garam masala, and coriander, then breaded in flour or cornstarch, and deep-fried. Chicken lollipops are usually served as an appetizer at Chinese restaurants in India.

India

Chicken 65

There are many origin stories about how chicken 65 got its name. Some claim that the chicken must be sixty-five days old to achieve optimal flavor; one legend has it that the original recipe had sixty-five ingredients; another holds that it takes sixty-five tries to get the dish right. Reading the Internet makes me want to put my money behind the idea that the dish was invented in 1965, either in military kitchens during the Indo-Pakistani War or at a hotel called Buhari in the city of Chennai, in southeast India, where the dish is most popular.

In any case, chicken 65 is delicious: thighs are chopped into pieces and marinated in some combination of MSG, Kashmiri chili powder, coriander, ginger-garlic paste, salt, and pepper. The pieces are coated in rice flour, cornstarch, or potato starch, dusted with more of the chili powder, and fried. Afterward, the pieces of fried chicken are sautéed in a spiced yogurt sauce made with green chili, cumin seeds, coriander, Kashmiri chili powder, curry leaves, ginger, and garlic.

China

La Zi Ji

La zi ji—chicken with chilies—is a specialty from the city of Chongqing, adjacent to Sichuan Province. Bone-in chicken is chopped into bite-size pieces, marinated in soy sauce, sugar, Shaoxing wine, ginger, and salt, and then deep-fried. The pile of chicken pieces are quickly stir-fried with tons of dried red chilies, garlic, and Sichuan peppercorns. The chilies are so numerous that, at the table, one needs to pick through the mountain of them, hunting for pieces of meat. (It is an amateur mistake to try to eat the chilies; they're there for aroma and garnish and flare—not sustenance.)

China

Zha Zi Ji

The Cleaver Quarterly *features long-form writing that covers Chinese food as a global phenomenon, in both print and online.*

Cantonese fried chicken (*zha zi ji*) has no use for batter. Like its northern cousin, Peking duck, it showcases a shatteringly crisp skin. The cooking process begins with the chicken being poached or steamed to infuse the meat with the flavors of scallion, ginger, Sichuan pepper, star anise, cinnamon, and fennel. Next, the skin is brushed with a maltose-vinegar glaze and left to dry overnight. Lastly, the bird is submerged in hot oil until the skin caramelizes into a red-gold glossy crunch, then served immediately.

For the sake of spectacle, the crisped chicken is occasionally presented whole—deep-fried cockscomb and all—but most diners expect a platter piled high with neatly hacked chunks, garnished with puffy curled shrimp crackers and a zesty pepper-salt for dipping.

Because the integrity of the skin requires that the bird remain whole through the deep-frying process, restaurants don't sell them piecemeal. You order a whole bird or nothing at all. Zha zi ji also happens to be Cantonese slang for any pop star who's on a hot streak. Apparently there's no better symbol for peak popularity than crispy fried chicken. Hard to argue with that.

—*The Cleaver Quarterly*

Taiwan

Yan Su Ji

Cathy Erway is the author of The Food of Taiwan *and* The Art of Eating In.

Much of Taiwan's street-food culture originated with food carts that lined up outside of temples so that worshippers could grab a bite after praying. One of the creations from that cart culture is now the signature fried chicken of the country: crunchy fried chicken with basil leaves. To make the dish, small pieces of chicken are marinated in a hearty amount of "fried salt and pepper chicken powder" (炸盐酥鸡粉), a condiment that's a mix of finely ground salt, white pepper, and five-spice powder. Garlic is usually added to the marinade, and a sweet-potato-flour dredge gives the chicken its signature super crunchy, crackly crust. This is typical street food, and it's often served in a paper bag steaming hot from the fryer, garnished with crisp and aromatic fried basil leaves.

— Cathy Erway

Japan

Conbini (Convenience Store) Chicken

Kee Byung-keun is a Korean-American writer living in Japan.

Let's just dispense with the obvious: Lawson has the best convenience-store fried chicken in Japan. First and foremost, it registers like it is really made from a chicken (as much as popcorn-sized bites of any animal can taste like itself). Secondly, its coating displays actual crispness. It's juicy without being greasy. It can be enjoyed in different flavors, like red pepper or cheese. And it comes in a cute little sleeve that fits perfectly in your hand while you cruise between Shibuya bars drunk out of your mind. With 7-Eleven or FamilyMart's chicken, you won't be so happy, even if you are equally intoxicated.

The shop closest to my apartment—and therefore the one subject to most of my poor late-night purchasing decisions—is a 7-Eleven. The crust is too rubbery on the outside and too greasy on the inside. I still leer at it every night as something viable, knowing full well that my hope will be transmuted to grief the second it is in my hand. The appeal is morbid.

But it's FamilyMart that offers me the greatest consternation. On a recent lunch break, I was sitting down to a *conbini* smorgasbord of rice balls, fried chicken, and bottled tea, but when I bit into the chicken, hot juice burst into my mouth and onto my hand. I pulled away and saw that my chicken was literally dripping with liquid. I was horrified. Was it fat? Was it meat juice? Did it even matter? Why was there so much of it?! I had no napkins, so in order to contain the mess, I thrust the chicken back into my mouth and sucked it down. More liquid dripped from the edges of my mouth. I felt sadness and despair, but mostly I just wished there were a Lawson nearby.

— Kee Byung-keun

La Zi Ji

Japan
Kara-age/Tatsuta-age

Kara-age (literally "tang fried") employs a Chinese-influenced method of frying that dates back to sometime before the eighteenth century. It specifically refers to dredging whatever you're frying in potato starch (or a mixture of potato starch and flour) to get a crisp, paper-thin skin.

Tatsuta-age is the most common type of kara-age, where bite-size pieces of chicken are marinated in soy sauce, sake, and ginger, dunked in potato starch, then fried. Sometimes, whole thighs are used instead—a rarity sometimes referred to as "big kara-age," or by another name entirely, *sanzoku-yaki*. Wings can also be fried, but this is not considered kara-age; they are instead called *tebasaki*.

My favorite way to eat kara-age is also maybe the trashiest—bowls of ramen topped with it. In Tokyo, there is this one place called Gachi that sells a *tsukemen* ramen topped with a whole fried thigh. Umakara Ramen Hyori does a gargantuan spicy *tonkotsu,* also topped with a thigh. And Kichijoji Donburi serves gonzo rice bowls, and the basic one comes with six fist-sized pieces of kara-age and way too much tartar sauce. Most people add extra kara-age, because if you're going to die you might as well die right.

—*Kee Byung-keun*

Japan
Toriten

Toriten is tempura chicken that originated in the early sixties in Oita Prefecture, and this is still where you'll most often find it, at street-side stands and in restaurants. The marinade for the chicken is nearly identical to kara-age, but toriten is battered à la tempura in a mixture of ice cold water, egg, and flour. Any part of the chicken can be cut into small pieces and used. Preferences about crispiness differ—some people don't mind letting the juices from the chicken soak through and dampen the outer layer. Those who prefer a crispier breading will double-fry the toriten. The chicken is served with ponzu, which, in its simplest form, is soy sauce cut with a sour citrus juice, like that of the *daidai,* a fruit similar to a Seville orange.

Korea

Corey Lee is the chef of Benu and In Situ in San Francisco.

To me there are two different kinds of Korean fried chicken. First there's *tong-dak,* which is the original fried chicken. It's traditionally dredged in sweetly seasoned rice flour, but other than that it's just plain fried chicken, served with radish pickles.

The newer version—the very, very crisp double-fried wings, often lacquered in some kind of sauce—started to proliferate in Seoul in the early nineties. Back then I'd go to Korea every summer, and on one trip my grandmother—who did not speak a lick of English—asked me if I wanted to go get some "chik-kin," because it was the cool new thing. Now it's spread around the world with chains like Bonchon and Kyo-Chon. As "Korean" as it is, to me, it's really a product of fusion. It's the combination of two Asian cultures—Korean flavors and Chinese cooking technique.

The multistep process-—cooking the wings, cooling them, then frying them in hot oil—is certainly something you find in Chinese cooking. One of the most exceptional chicken wings I've ever had was at Celebrity Cuisine in Hong Kong, where they cooked the wings, cooled them, stuffed them with bird's nest, and then deep-fried them. All the moisture trying to escape the bird's nest puffed up like crazy, and the skin crisped like Peking duck in the deep-fryer.

Though the Chinese will often put a whole chicken through the same technique, it's really ideal for chicken wings because of the way the skin completely encapsulates the meat. On the second pass, the steam trapped inside the jacket of skin will keep the meat moist and the fat will render out, ideally leaving nothing to the skin but crisp crunch. (I'll note that the first cooking doesn't need to be in a deep-fryer, but if you have one going, there's no reason you wouldn't use it.)

After the wings get fried, they get glazed, and that's what most people think of as Korean fried chicken today. They're for eating on a night out, while drinking. Tongdak, simple fried chicken, is the sort of thing you might eat with whatever *banchan* you have lying around at home.

—*Corey Lee*

Nigeria

Chinelo Onwualu is a writer and editor living in Abuja, Nigeria.

Fried chicken is well known in Nigeria today, but this wasn't always the case. While it was sometimes part of a big Sunday family dinner, it has never held the same status as other dishes, like *jollof* rice. It began rising in the country's collective regard in the nineties through the fast-food outlets styled after Kentucky Fried Chicken—Tastee Fried Chicken and Mr. Bigg's are two chains common in big cities around Nigeria and Africa, respectively. The chickens are typically marinated in Maggi seasoning, bay leaves, and *yaji* (a traditional spice mix of black, white, and red peppercorns, salt, ginger, clove, and dried chilies) before being dredged and fried. Fried chicken is widely considered an expensive treat, much like pizza or ice cream, and not to be consumed regularly.

—Chinelo Onwualu

Kenyan Chicken and Chips

Sandra Zhao writes about food and bakes cupcakes in Nairobi, Kenya.

Chicken Inn, Maryland Chicken, McFrys, Chicken Roost, Nyammy Chicken Inn: all of these are restaurants in Nairobi where you can pop in and walk out five minutes later with a worryingly thin plastic bag filled with steaming-hot fried chicken and chips.

Most of these restaurants are simply corridors: cashier and fryer on one side, a long, narrow counter with stools opposite it. There's often a wall-to-wall mirror where you can watch yourself and your neighbors as you collectively scarf. Salt-shakers abound, malt vinegar is common, and there are almost always bottles of Peptang tomato sauce (a neon-red cousin of Heinz) and Peptang hot and sweet sauce (a distant relative of an imitation of a chili). You might find an actual bottle of Heinz, though usually it's watered down or filled with Peptang.

For a non-fried but equally popular chicken experience, there's *kuku choma*. The chicken is slathered in oil and thrown on the grill until it's charred and the skin is crisp. Stop by any choma joint—identifiable by the window of meat hanging on hooks—and take a seat. Someone will come by with a water pitcher and soap for you to wash your hands, and the chicken will soon follow on a wooden board along with a little pile of salt, *ugali* (steamed ground maize), and *kachumbari* (chopped tomatoes and onions, seasoned with lime juice and sometimes cilantro).

You can find both chicken and chips and kuku choma joints across the country; in cities they're popular among the middle class for lunch or a late-night bite. In more rural areas, chicken is a special meal, and chicken and chips or kuku choma might be a celebratory outing with family or friends.

—Sandra Zhao

Italy

Pollo Fritto alla Toscana

Tuscan fried chicken comes from a centuries-old Jewish custom, wherein it's served for Hanukkah. As is true of nearly everything food related, preparations vary by region and even from town to town.

Generally speaking, the chicken is marinated in lemon juice, garlic, thyme, and nutmeg, then coated in egg, dredged in flour, and fried in olive oil. It's served topped with fried herbs, like sage and oregano, and fried artichoke hearts. (Sometimes, cut-up chicken is fried right along with the artichokes.)

Ukraine/
France/America

Chicken Kiev

Despite its name, chicken Kiev has its roots in France, where in the 1840s, chefs to the Russian royalty traveled for inspiration and saw a version of the dish being made with veal. They returned home and started making it with chicken, which was cheaper and easier to find. They called the imported dish "Mikhailovska cutlet," and it was served in fancy dining rooms.

In the U.S., when influxes of immigrants from the Soviet Union arrived, New York restaurants like the Russian Tea Room began serving the dish with a new name: chicken Kiev. American tourists in the former USSR started requesting it, which led to its increased popularity there. And now it's become largely passé everywhere.

In the classic dish, a chicken cutlet is pounded down, coated in egg and bread crumbs, rolled up around a filling of butter and herbs, and pan-fried. American versions of the dish call for garlic and parsley, and Russian versions call for cheese. Some chefs in Ukraine insist on using only butter.

Chicken Milanese

Milanese/ Milanesa/ Schnitzel

The breaded chicken cutlet—most often a piece of breast meat pounded thin and fried after a trip through some kind of egg-flour-bread dredge—pops up as a diet destroyer in so many places around the world, it feels wrong to assign it a particular provenance.

My mind travels first to Eastern Europe, to schnitzel country, the place where the Danube flows. I know veal and pork are the first meats of schnitzel, but the schnitzeling of a chicken is a worthy way to turn cottony meat into velvet. The magic of the schnitzel is forged in a crucible of butter: cooked in a bath of it, the chef spooning it over the cutlet in a golden cascade until the crust is crisped but tender and rich, the same as the meat within. Sour cucumber salads and a wedge of lemon might be nearby to lend it some acid. They will be aided, abetted, and made better by the assist of a beguiling white wine with a word like SCHEUREBE scrawled across the bottle.

Up in Poland matzo meal might be the breading element; the same could be said for some of the schnitzel you'd find in Israel, but bread crumbs are common just about everywhere. I've heard tell of Yemeni schnitzel seasoned with *hawayij*—a blend of black pepper, caraway, saffron, cardamom, and turmeric—but never had the pleasure of eating it.

If we head west, we can plan a stopover in Milan for *cotoletta alla milanese*. Much like in schnitzel country, pigs and baby cows are more likely to have their flesh mallet-tenderized and cooked in butter than chickens, but any beast who befalls that delicious fate will find a bit of parmesan cheese brought to the party, and maybe the earthy kiss of sage in the butter. More importantly, perhaps, than the fried meat itself is the way the name of the city attached itself to fried chicken cutlets in points far southwest.

In many of the Spanish-speaking parts of the Americas, ordering a *milanesa de pollo* will get you some manner of pounded and fried chicken. Limes will supplant lemons in the acid department. In Mexico, a milanesa can end up anywhere a cook puts it—on a plate with rice and beans and the like—but the most classic way to have it is in a fried chicken sandwich, or *torta de milanesa*. They are sold in *tortarias* all over Mexico, but they originated in the city of Puebla, where there are whole marketplaces devoted to the sandwich.

There, the cutlet gets sandwiched in a *cemita*, a dense, slightly sweet, brioche-like seeded roll. The sandwich is dressed with black-bean paste, Oaxacan cheese, avocado, chilies in adobo, lettuce, and perhaps a sprinkling of fresh herbs. *Pápalo* is one of the herbs; whenever I eat it I make a face like a cat licking a freshly Windexed window, but somehow it works in the torta, giving it that however you say *je ne sais quoi* in Spanish.

Alex Raij, the chef of a spate of Spanish restaurants in New York City (including the Michelin-starred La Vara), said her favorite dish growing up was the *milanesa de pollo a la napolitana*. She calls it "a next-level chicken parm": a cutlet is breaded and fried, and then baked with cheese and tomato. It's popular both in restaurants and in home cooking in Argentina, she told us, and is frequently served to children.

In the United States, we put fried chicken on salad—I remember my surprise in learning that Caesar salads don't always come with a fingers-on option—but if there is a cutlet that reigns supreme in the land of the red, white, and blue, well, it might be hard to say which it is. In the South, it's going in a soft bun a quarter of its size, maybe with some pickles. In the middle of the country, that fried chicken might get smothered in gravy and set up with some mashed potatoes and peas. But in many places it's gonna meet up with mozzarella and tomato sauce and go great with a Scorsese movie. Usually we call that a "chicken parm," but its lineage almost certainly tracks to southern Italy, not Parma.

Let's end this tour of flat-fried chickens in the land of the rising sun, where we must tip our hats to chicken *katsu*, fried chicken cutlets breaded in jackets of jaggedly crisp panko crumbs. While there are probably as many ways to eat chicken katsu as there are ways to dress up for a Sailor Moon cosplay party, the one that seems the most quintessentially Japanese to me is chicken curry katsu—a pile of white rice topped with a thinly sliced, crispy fried cutlet that is ensconced in a tar-pit-thick spill of deep brown and slightly sweet Japanese curry. There will be raw cabbage to add crunch, there will be beer to wash it down, and there will be heartburn to follow.

—*Peter Meehan*

The Americas

Pollo Campero

Pollo Campero, a Central American fast-food-chicken restaurant, opened in 1971 in Guatemala City. Today, there are over three hundred locations worldwide, including more than sixty-five U.S. outposts. While Pollo Campero's recipe is one of those closely guarded corporate secrets, its flavor recalls orange juice, annatto paste, garlic powder, and bay leaf. The crust is made with flour and bread crumbs, which renders the chicken perfectly crispy and juicy without being greasy. It's a solid fast-food-variety fried chicken, and the empanadas and fried plantains you can get alongside are welcome accompaniments.

Brazil

Coxinha

The name means "little thigh," but coxinhas are actually croquettes of shredded chicken enveloped in dough that's formed into the shape of a chicken thigh, breaded, and fried. "Coxinha is also a nickname for people who dress really posh but actually have no class whatsoever, and who would never eat coxinha because they'd consider it peasant food," says chef Alberto Landgraf of the late Michelin-starred Epice in São Paulo.

As legend goes, this dish was invented in the late nineteenth century for one of Princess Isabel's sons. This son had very particular eating habits, and would eat only chicken thighs. One day the cook was out of thighs, but had some leftover meat from a feast the night before. To stretch what she had, she wrapped the meat in dough, breaded it, and fried it. The prince loved it, and the dish grew in fame throughout the village, and eventually the country.

"The base of the dough changes, varying from potatoes to just plain flour, and—the best one for me—manioc [cassava]," Landgraf says. "Once, some of my cooks went to a dodgy *boteco* (casual Brazilian drink-and-snack spot) late after service, and one of them asked for a coxinha. After biting into it, he said it tasted sour, so he asked the server if the cooks had put lemon zest in the dough, and the server said, '*Lemon zest? What the fuck is that? It's probably just off because it's been sitting out since yesterday morning.*'"

Brazil

Frango à Passarinho

Frango à passarinho is a tapas-style dish that you'll find at botecos in the southern and southeastern parts of the country. It's served with cold beer. "It's called 'à passarinho' (little bird) because the chicken is chopped into small pieces that resemble the small birds eaten in the countryside," says Landgraf.

The dish can be made with chicken wings or with a whole chicken that's diced up, bones and all. Either way, the pieces are marinated in lime, salt, and garlic, sometimes breaded in flour, and then fried. The finished dish gets topped with lots of chopped garlic and occasionally chopped herbs like parsley. Landgraf says some of the best versions of frango à passarinho can be found at Japanese *izakayas* around Brazil, and says he likes to specially request pieces with more skin and fat attached to them.

United States of America

Southern Fried Chicken

In the South, everyone's mother has a slightly different recipe for fried chicken, and all of them make it best. All aspects of the cooking process are up for debate, but generally, the chicken is cut into frying pieces at the bone (thigh, drumstick, wing, breast), soaked in buttermilk, dredged in flour mixed with seasonings (these vary, but pepper, garlic powder, paprika, and cayenne are all common), and deep-fried, most commonly in lard or peanut oil.

Fried chicken in America exists at the intersection of European and West African tradition. "Chickens were fried at some point in England, and the notion of fried chicken would have come from the English settlers. Then there is a certain kind of African mastery of frying in deep oil, and I think the two intersected in a kind of way," says Dr. Jessica Harris, a food scholar and professor at Queens College, CUNY, and the author of numerous books on the food of the African diaspora.

In early America, chicken was a fancy dish; wealthy white plantation owners ate it, and likely used recipes for fricassee—a dish of braised chicken—influenced by European tradition. "Chicken would have been a once-a-year occurrence, if even that, during the time of enslavement," Harris says. African slaves were the ones doing the cooking on plantations, and since they, too, had a fried chicken tradition, they undoubtedly borrowed from their own background.

The advancement of the railroad system in the late nineteenth century encouraged the growth of the chicken industry, and the number of chickens in America more than doubled. "What happens in the African-American world once chicken becomes more widespread and cheap—though this isn't monolithic—is you get people who are using fried chicken to create, if not wealth, then at least income," Harris says. "You've got those chicken ladies Psyche Williams-Forson writes about so eloquently in *Building Houses out of Chicken Legs*, who are selling fried chicken to passengers in railroad stations, which serves as a kind of early example of fast-food fried chicken. It's here that you get the whole notion of fried chicken as an expertise of African Americans, that is then used for entrepreneurship."

United States of America

Kentucky Fried Chicken

Harland Sanders was a middle-school dropout and a veteran from Indiana. In the 1930s, he opened a restaurant in the service station he operated, selling Southern food like fried chicken. After a successful two decades, he franchised Kentucky Fried Chicken to a man from Salt Lake City named Peter Harman. Sanders closed his original restaurant three years later when the construction of a new highway diverted traffic away from his service station. He spent the rest of his life visiting KFC locations across the country. KFC has grown quickly abroad, especially in China, where the company has over five thousand restaurants.

Everyone talks about KFC's original recipe, but what's actually crucial to the product—and fast-food fried chicken in general—is the pressure fryer. If it sounds dangerous, it's because it is, but the process of pressure frying allowed fried chicken to cook quickly and efficiently. A commercially viable pressure fryer wasn't invented until 1957, and now, fast-food restaurants use a safer, more finely tuned version of the original machine.

United States of America

Buffalo Wings

In a now-famous 1980 *New Yorker* article, Calvin Trillin investigates whether Anchor Bar, in Buffalo, New York, is indeed the ancestral home of the buffalo wing, as everyone, including the residents of Buffalo, proclaim them to be. Teressa Bellissimo, chef and co-owner of Anchor Bar, first made the wing in the 1960s either as a way to use a mistaken shipment of wings (the restaurant traditionally received necks and backs, which were used for the spaghetti sauce) or to please a group of big-spending customers—stories vary. And in the end, Trillin isn't convinced that the Anchor Bar can be credited for deep-fried chicken wings, considering that black people have been eating them for centuries.

Regardless of its origin, the wing became tremendously popular, and soon made its way onto the Anchor Bar's regular menu, and menus all over town. Now it's served at bars all over the country, where the wings are covered in Frank's hot sauce (often mixed with a load of melted butter) and served with celery and blue-cheese dipping sauce.

United States of America

Fried Chicken and Waffles

In its most popular form, chicken and waffles consists of bone-in fried chicken served with a waffle, syrup, and Tabasco sauce. However, the true origins of chicken and waffles are difficult to discern, as John T. Edge notes in his book *Fried Chicken: An American Story*. The dish is variously credited to Roscoe's, a restaurant in Los Angeles, Wells Supper Club in Harlem, and home cooks in the South. The most widely circulated story is that the dish is linked to the 1930s Harlem Renaissance, when musicians and artists would frequent Wells Supper Club, the twenty-four-hour restaurant that served breakfast, lunch, and dinner. "It's the coming together of the early-morning breakfast and the late-night dinner," Harris says. Wells offered its chicken during the breakfast service that began at midnight, where it shared a menu with breakfast staples like waffles.

Buffalo Wings

United States of America

Nashville Hot Chicken

Nashville hot chicken was famously invented in the restaurant Prince's in Nashville in the 1930s. The irresistible but apocryphal legend is that the dish was conceived as punishment for infidelity: after realizing her boyfriend was out late philandering, Thornton Prince's unnamed girlfriend attempted to burn his mouth off by dumping copious amounts of spice in his Sunday morning chicken. The plan backfired, as Prince loved the chicken and perfected the recipe for his eventual restaurant. Prince's still serves hot chicken, and it's still family run. In the past decade or so, the dish's popularity has taken off: KFC has added it to their menus, and restaurants like Hattie B's have gone into business as hot chicken specialists.

To make hot chicken, the bird is quartered or cut into pieces at the bone, like Southern fried chicken, dry-brined in salt and pepper, and fried with the bone in. After frying, it is sauced in a searing mixture of cayenne, garlic powder, paprika, and oil or lard. The chicken is served on top of a piece of white bread, which soaks up the drippings and provides a promise of relief from the heat. But, especially when you attempt anything more than mild Nashville hot chicken, there is no relief to be found—just psychedelically spicy chicken-fried pain.

Nashville Hot Chicken

United States of America

General Tso's Chicken

General Tso (actual name: Zuo Zongtang) was a real historical figure, but he did not invent the miracle chicken. Zuo was a famous military leader who died in 1885, but the chicken that was named after him was not invented until the 1950s. The real inventor of the dish is Peng Chang-kuei. After the Chinese civil war, Peng moved to Taiwan with the leaders of the defeated Nationalist Party. He'd studied under the famous chef for the party, Cao Jingchen, and eventually became the head chef for the Nationalist Party banquets.

In the early seventies, Peng moved to New York City and brought an early iteration of what would become General Tso's chicken with him when he opened a restaurant on Fourth Street in New York City. The original version of General Tso's did not contain sugar and was more traditionally Hunanese in flavor. Sugar was eventually added to appease the American palate, and its popularity took off across the country. Modern versions now consist of cubed pieces of meat that are coated in egg, starch, and soy sauce, then fried in peanut oil. They get tossed with fried garlic, ginger, chilies, and an ooey-gooey sauce of cornstarch, tomato paste, vinegar, soy sauce, and sugar.

Peng brought the dish with him when he moved back to his hometown of Changsha, the capital of Hunan Province, and opened a restaurant with it on the menu. But while it's eaten all over the world, General Tso's chicken remains mostly unknown in the area, according to Fuchsia Dunlop's *Revolutionary Chinese Cookbook*. **LP**

The Big Chicken

By Gillian Ferguson
Photograph by Johnathon Kelso

The Big Chicken is a fifty-six-foot-tall slab of metal parked on the edge of a suburban highway in the town of Marietta, Georgia. Its boxy silhouette is more Bauhaus than barnyard, and if it weren't for the cockscomb-red paint job, beady eyes, and animatronic beak silently squawking at the traffic below, you might never recognize it as fowl.

Chicken looms large in Georgia, the number one state in chicken slaughter. And like so much of the South's history, when you peel back the layers of something as mindlessly joyful as a five-story cock, out comes the long shadow of Dixie. The Big Chicken was built in 1963 to lure passersby to Johnny Reb's Chick-Chuck-'N'-Shake, a fried-chicken shack with twenty-one-piece "barrel" boxes and a name that harkened back to the Confederacy. (Johnny Reb, short for Rebel, was the name ascribed to Confederate soldiers.) Atlanta's Johnny Reb restaurants were known for displaying Confederate decor and hosting nightly performances of Confederate battle songs, making a larger-than-life bird seem like a fairly innocuous piece of flair.

In 1974, the Chick-Chuck-'N'-Shake became a KFC, and the corporation (whose founder had his own sordid past with segregationist politics) almost tore the structure down. But the bird's life was spared, and in 2016, *USA Today* named the Big Chicken Georgia's most iconic landmark, ranking it alongside the Grand Canyon in Arizona and Glacier National Park in Montana.

Unlike those places of natural beauty, or bigger engineering feats like the Golden Gate Bridge in California, the Big Chicken is a landmark because it's a weird bit of novelty architecture, so uncharacteristic in a sprawl of suburban sameness that radio ads give directions using it as a landmark. It isn't a destination; it's something you pass on the way to somewhere else.

Bernard Baff and the Kosher Killers

A Tale of Birds and Blood in Turn-of-the-Century New York

By Tove Danovich   Illustrations by Pete Sharp

At the turn of the twentieth century, New York City's Live Poultry Commission Merchants' Protective Association thought they had fixed every inch of the city's kosher poultry market in their favor. They paid off the wholesale jobbers and bought up nearly every stall in the West Washington Market. At the start of each week, they held meetings to decide what price the city's Jewish residents should pay to get their kosher chicken. Whenever an aspiring poultry merchant tried to break the trust, they handed him a wad of cash as encouragement to find another calling. If someone needed more than cash to be convinced, the association might poison his horses as a warning.

In July 1913, Joe Cohen, a higher-up in the association, thought that Bernard Baff, who'd left the association and gone freelance, might be in need of a good scare. He found a group of Italian gangsters who were willing to drive to Baff's house in Arverne, Queens, and put a bomb on the veranda. The bomb was a dud, the first of many failed attempts to scare the illiterate immigrant, who was often proclaimed the "poultry king" of America's biggest metropolis.

NEW APPETITES, NEW OPPORTUNITIES

Until massive waves of Jewish immigrants arrived in 1880, New York City didn't eat much chicken: its stockyards and stomachs were filled with beef and pork, along with the occasional mutton. A representative 1859 menu from the Metropolitan Hotel listed twenty-three options containing beef or pork but only two choices for chicken—tying the bird with mackerel in popularity. But Jewish immigrants, fleeing the anti-Semitism of Eastern European countries, brought kosher diets with them and a tradition of eating chicken for Friday's Shabbat dinner.

From the late 1800s to 1916, the annual sales of live poultry went from 25 million pounds to "almost five times that amount," according to a New York trade journal. By the 1880s, sixty thousand Jews lived in the twenty-block square known as the Lower East Side. By 1910, the Jewish population had increased from roughly 4 percent of the city's population to almost a full quarter—and everyone wanted a kosher chicken.

In 1889, the tan-brick structure of the West Washington Market in what is known today as the Meatpacking District was unveiled. Its merchants sold meat, poultry, or dairy using new technology that could run brine water through 2,500 feet of pipes, keeping cold-storage rooms between 25 and 45 degrees. The majority of New York's live poultry industry soon concentrated in this market, where they received ten to fifteen train cars of live poultry every week. The steel railcars were specially outfitted for hauling live poultry and could each hold up to twenty thousand pounds of squawking birds. The chickens were housed in containers that went eight levels high, with only enough space left for a narrow corridor for feed storage and a living area for the unlucky carman whose job it was to watch the birds over the days spent on the rails and waiting at terminals.

Shippers sold their birds on commission to wholesale receivers, mostly association members. At the association's height of power, they controlled nearly all of the birds brought into New York City. In 1908, the Pennsylvania Railroad delivered 902 cars of live poultry, 91 percent of which went to association members—they received over 14 million pounds of chicken and other birds from that rail line alone. These receivers were effectively the sole distributors of poultry for the city's retail slaughtermen and butchers. Some of them even double-dipped into the retail market.

When Baff arrived from the Pale of Settlement—the only part of the Russian Empire where Jews were allowed to live at the time—there was no Ellis Island or Statue of Liberty waiting to greet him in New York. Those would come later. What Baff found was a city of 1.3 million people and a new life free from restrictions. He entered the butchering trade and ran a shop of his own for nearly nine years before deciding that live poultry was where the real money could be made. He opened his first live-chicken business at 60 Thompson Avenue. By then he'd wised up: he dissociated himself from the association and, freed from their price-fixing scheme, decided to undersell his competition and make up in

volume what he lost in price. He owned the chickens and he owned a kosher slaughterhouse, so he could undercut other poultrymen in the chicken-meat market. Plus, he mastered the art of "overcropping."

Overcropping was the poultryman's way of tipping the scales in his favor, quite literally. Baff first arranged for his chickens to be starved for a day or two prior to their arrival. Just before they were weighed for sale, the birds were encouraged to gorge themselves on an all-you-can-peck buffet. Baff was rumored to have mixed gravel and small rocks into the feed for added weight. The practice was called overcropping, because it packed the chicken's digestive area known as the crop. It was so widespread that some estimates say chicken-buying New Yorkers were paying for something in the range of 150,000 to 300,000 pounds of sand and gravel every week.

By the early 1910s, Baff, who hadn't even been in business for a decade, was the most hated man in an industry that wished it were as good at cheating as he was.

In 1910 two members of the association, Pauline Jacobs and Charles Werner, tried to use the justice system to get at Baff: they sued him for nonpayment. Like most people facing a lawsuit, Baff hired a lawyer—unlike most, he and his lawyer went straight to the district attorney's office and spilled the beans about the association's shady dealings. Baff agreed to become the state's star witness in a circus of a case that captured public attention around the world.

Thirteen of the eighty-seven indicted poultrymen were sentenced. The district attorney, Charles Whitman, called their acts "sordid and mean and contemptible and despicable." He continued: "[The poultrymen] did not control gigantic enterprises, but as far as they could, they deliberately extorted money from those who, under the conditions, were about as little able to pay as any in the land."

In its final judgments, the court said, "A conspiracy to monopolize and control

a food product is a mean and insidious crime stealthily committed and usually, if not always, by men who masquerade in the garb of good repute, but in whose breasts the quality of common morality has been stifled by the most despicable form of greed."

Despite the fact that Baff was guilty of many of the same illegal schemes, his stand against the association made him a hero. During the trial, his attorney flaunted that Baff had been fighting the organization since 1910 while downplaying that he had once been a member.

The Sherman antitrust law, the first federal act to outlaw monopolistic practices, was passed in 1890. Nine years after the

Sherman Act, New York developed the Donnelly Act. The association had the dubious honor of being the first trust successfully prosecuted by that legislation, and several of its members were the first men in the nation to be jailed for anticompetitive activities.

VILLAINY COMES CHEAP

In 1913, Antonio Cardinale and his brother-in-law purchased a retail chicken market on 108th Street, hoping to make their fortune. Business wasn't good. Being an Italian in the kosher-chicken industry was difficult. Jewish vendors were wary of selling to him and, unlike Baff, Cardinale couldn't post in the Jewish paper every week to advertise his low prices. As if things weren't hard enough, Baff's friend and customer Aaron Newmark had a shop around the corner on 109th Street. Newmark, Cardinale said, was buying six or maybe seven cars a week from Baff. Newmark was helping Baff "ruin the business up there and something ought to be done."

Joe Cohen, the association leader who'd originally tried to bomb Baff, picked up the torch from there. "This man will never behave himself. He has got to be killed. He will ruin the business of everybody," Cohen told Cardinale.

New York had cleaned up slightly in the half century since the rowdy heyday of the Five Points, when gangs like the Bowery Boys and Dead Rabbits ran wild, but most new Jewish immigrants still lived in poverty in the tenements of lower Manhattan. The early 1900s were the beginning of an era for Jewish crime and gangsters. Arson and horse poisoning were crimes that were "associated almost exclusively with New York's Jews," wrote Dr. Jenna Weissman Joselit in *Our Gang,* a history of Jewish crime and community in the Big Apple.

For one hundred dollars, you could commission a hit man from the local saloon to shoot someone; shooting to kill might cost you five hundred dollars. Police Commissioner Arthur Woods said that it might take as little as ten dollars to have someone knocked down and stomped on. "Of course," Commissioner Woods said, "if it were a man who could stir up a fuss, the price would be higher." Baff wasn't just hard to oust, but wealthy, too. Putting a price on his head was costly.

Attempts to scare or kill Baff failed one after another. The association hired gangsters to shoot Baff on the street but could never get him alone; his son Harry was always by his side. The owner of the safe-house saloon, Ippolito Greco tried getting two young thugs to use a "poisoned ice pick" on Baff. It's unclear which of the many things wrong with this plan caused it to fall through.

The association eventually bought a .22 Winchester rifle with a silencer and set a gunman to wait in a loft of association poultryman Charles Hawk's office in the West Washington Market. He'd have a straight shot at Baff if he came walking past. Days went by, and the gunman continued waiting. He fired off practice shots when no one was around. Finally he conceded defeat. He told his employers that Baff had never showed up—with four stores in Manhattan and Brooklyn to tend to as well as additional locations in Boston and Philadelphia, Baff was a busy man—but he was wrong. Baff had walked past multiple times. The hit man, hired from the local saloon, had simply failed to recognize him.

The cumulative effect of all these murder attempts was putting a strain on Cohen's wallet. In the summer of 1914, New York poultrymen pooled their funds to avert a strike by chicken pullers and handlers, which was scheduled to occur just prior to the Jewish holidays, when it would do the most damage to business. The merchants got together to contribute between five and fifty dollars per person—Baff himself may have contributed twenty-five dollars. The strike never took place. Most who added to the fund probably assumed the funds had worked as promised and bought the necessary goodwill from the strikers. Unbeknownst to all but a few, the funds were never meant to end a strike. Instead, it was part of an anti-Baff fund that would pay the killers who would end Baff's life.

Baff was still at work when he received a messenger. It was November 24, 1914—two days before Thanksgiving. The sun had set, and the night was neither warmer nor colder than anyone would expect in November. No one knows what ruse was employed to get Baff alone and away from his office. Whatever it was, it worked. Baff greeted the visitor and, soon after, left his son Harry in the shop they owned together. The Poultry King turned north on Thirteenth Avenue (now the Chelsea Piers). He was just passing the Brooklyn Poultry Co. when two men stepped out of a darkened doorway behind him.

The gunmen shot simultaneously. Two bullets hit Baff in the back at close range and went through his body as he fell. Some witnesses reported hearing him cry, "I am shot!"

After escaping bombs, threats, and poisoned ice picks, Baff toppled to the ground. An ambulance arrived quickly to the scene, but it was too late. Bernard Baff was fifty-two years old when he died.

Onlookers described seeing two men leap over Baff's body and run south through the crowded streets. They got into a waiting car with a chauffeur in the driver's seat. People tried to run after the murderers, shouting at them as they sped off in their coffee-colored getaway car. Later reports said the car may have been stolen from one of Baff's associates. Somewhere between the crime scene and wherever the killer's next destination was—likely Greco's Harlem saloon—the men tossed their guns out of the moving car.

The district attorney's office saw the poultryman's death as an attack against the law itself. It was witness intimidation, the type of fixing Tammany Hall had been known for, and those charged with the safety of New York City's residents wanted it to stop. Mayor John P. Mitchel described Baff as "a peaceable, law-abiding citizen and respectable businessman of substantial means, who was not unmindful of the interests of the general public in the conduct of his private business." Mitchel continued, "If such a man can be wantonly done to death by hired thugs, then no merchant is safe who arouses the enmity of unscrupulous rivals."

The police prioritized finding Baff's killers. Mayor Mitchel said, "I should like to see all of these professional thugs driven

off the ends of the piers into the river." The Poultry King was one of twenty-five people who died in New York on November 24, 1914. But he was the only one whose murder trial was regularly news in national and international papers for almost a full decade afterward.

The city remained outraged.

"[Baff] lived in the shadow of the automatic gun because he would not subscribe to the principle that in the West Washington market there is no law but the law of force, no property right that may not be violated by workers more criminal than industrious, and nobody to pay the bills of wholesale loot, theft and fraud but the ultimate public," wrote one particularly feeling reporter for *The Day*. "He fought his fight right there in the midst of the criminalism and moral debauchery of the poultry market; fought with the weapons that he knew and so valiantly and successfully that they had to kill him to beat him."

Beginning with confessions from lower-level thugs, the police pieced together the team that was culpable for Baff's demise. The association had paid fifteen hundred dollars for the final act that killed Baff. The chauffer got two hundred fifty dollars.

One of the shooters, a young Italian by the name of Giuseppe Archiello, received only one hundred dollars. Two other brothers involved in the plan got three hundred dollars apiece. Two hundred dollars was split between miscellaneous go-betweens for their trouble and silence. Cardinale wasn't paid for the crime, though some speculated that Cohen may have promised to back a new business enterprise, and later said that his conscience was troubled by the murder and his role in it.

In 1916, Archiello and the driver of the getaway car were sent to Sing Sing to await the electric chair. Two years later, Joseph Cohen was also convicted for the murders and sentenced to death. Cardinale, who was brought back from Italy to testify in the murder trial, was never charged. All together, eleven men were indicted for their part in the murder. Greco died before the case went to trial.

The DA's office thought they had the case wrapped up when the unthinkable happened: one of their key witnesses, Joseph Sorro, said he'd made up much of his testimony.

In 1922, Cohen and the other association members had their sentences commuted. Cohen said, "I have hoped for the opportunity to vindicate myself. I think I can do that, and that I will never return here." Though the state had the option of retrying Cohen, they did not. No one else was ever charged with Baff's murder. Sorro, however, was given ten to twenty years for his perjured testimony.

Cohen wasn't a free man for long. In April 1932, three unidentified gunmen shot him as he was leaving his home in Brooklyn. The case didn't get much notice, and the killers were never found. Call it karma or simple coincidence in the often-violent business world of New York City chicken.

Baff died a hero for the common man, a lone voice against the trusts, but his death did nothing to strip the industry of its base tendencies. Only two years after his death, the state held an inquiry into the live-poultry market. This time, they alleged that B. Baff & Sons—with B. Baff no longer in the picture—were controlling the poultry market in Manhattan, Brooklyn, and the Bronx. The overcropping scam continued. During Passover in 1916, it was estimated that people paid $164,062 for 656,250 pounds of old food and rocks that the chickens had gobbled up before sale. LP

Kung

Fu

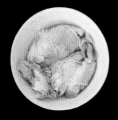
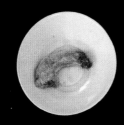

Chicken

ONE CHICKEN EATEN
IN NINE WAYS

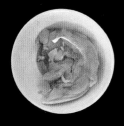

By Fuchsia Dunlop

Photographs by
Ian Cumming

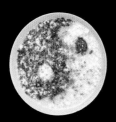
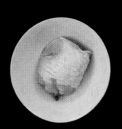

一鸡九吃

一鸡九吃是淮阴特级厨师王素华的教学示范菜。此菜很有典型意义。对烹饪操作过程中合理利用原材料具有参考作用。

鸡的分档及各菜组合见图5。

It was the diagram that did it.

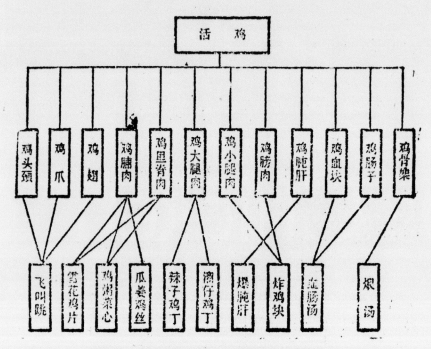

图5 鸡的分档及各菜组合示意图

烹调方法：煮、煸熘、炸、炒等多种。

【原料】

仔鸡1只	1500～2000克	鸡 蛋	4只
肥膘肉	100克	熟火腿末	25克
熟火腿小片	25克	熟冬笋	100克
水发香菇	100克	荸荠(马蹄)	25克
酱黄瓜	1条	酱生姜	25克
红大椒	2只	青菜叶	2张

Flicking through a cooking-school textbook I'd been given by a chef in Yangzhou, my eye was drawn to a fantastically complicated illustration. It was like a family tree: at the top of the lineage was a live chicken, with ruled lines showing how it could be divided into twelve descendant parts, which would, in turn and in various combinations, yield nine different dishes that could be served at a single meal. A headnote explained that *yi ji jiu chi* (one chicken eaten in nine ways) was a demonstration dish devised by Wang Suhua, a high-ranking chef specializing in Huaiyang cuisine, the grand, classical style of cooking in the old city of Yangzhou.

Chef Wang had designed each recipe to showcase his skill and the particular qualities of individual parts of the bird. There were appetizers, stir-fries, two soups, and some Chinese-style chicken nuggets. Textures ranged from chewy to custardy, from succulent to crisp. Technically, the dishes demanded mastery of the key skills of the Chinese professional kitchen: *dao gong* (knife work), *tiao wei* (the mixing of flavors), and *huo hou* (the command of heat). Every dish had to look, taste, and feel different from every other in order to conjure up a suitably enticing variety from a single principal ingredient.

Like any classically trained Chinese chef, Wang had started by contemplating his ingredients. He had analyzed their strengths and weaknesses and worked out ways to enhance the former and subdue the latter, choosing his seasonings and cooking methods accordingly. The bony head, feet, and wings have what my father would call a "high grapple factor": the kind of intricacy of cartilage and bones that the Chinese adore, so they are simply boiled and dressed, so they can be gnawed and chewed and enjoyed in all their textural complexity. The succulent flesh of the thighs is showcased by a quick velveting and stir-frying, while the smooth, boneless breast meat is both stir-fried and, in two other dishes, magicked into a silken paste. And because any Chinese chef knows that viscera such as gizzard and liver become leathery when overcooked, they are thinly sliced and swiftly flash-fried, with seasonings that smooth away any coarseness of flavor. The intestines are only fleetingly scalded, to preserve their sprightly slipperiness. The result of such thoughtful cooking is a whole meal of dazzling beauty and variety.

It was exhausting just reading the recipes, but for me, the challenge was irresistible. "One chicken nine ways" summed up one of the aspects I love most about Chinese cuisine: the combination of careful economy and deranged imagination. How sensible to ensure that when you take the life of a bird, virtually nothing is wasted besides claws and feathers. And how insane it is to spend hours dissecting it and transforming it into nine exquisite little dishes, when a typical Englishwoman would just shove it whole into the oven!

Of course, my first problem was finding a live chicken. With most dishes, any old dead chicken will do, but with this set of recipes, I needed not only flesh and bone but also very specific innards. Some London butchers or farmers' markets are able to provide a bag of giblets, but even the most adventurous English giblets would never include a chicken's intestines (you can't even buy chicken intestines in my favorite Chinatown supermarket, which stocks chicken hearts and gizzards). Moreover, one of Chef Wang's dishes required jellied chicken blood, which would be even more impossible to source. My only hope of obtaining jellied chicken blood in London would be to prepare it after slitting the throat of the bird myself.

I made a few calls, but my usual meat suppliers were unable to provide a bird that wasn't what they called "oven ready." Reckoning that it would be easier to find a live farmhouse bird in the countryside, I asked

my photographer friend Ian, who lives in a Cambridgeshire village, if he could track one down. The first farmer he called had plenty of chickens but was unwilling to sell them live: "We used to sell live chickens," said the woman he spoke with, "but then Asians kept buying them and killing them in their back gardens." Ian kept very quiet at this point. The second farmer had no such qualms, and Ian was able to buy a bird of suitable weight (about four and a half pounds) and bring her with him to London. Neither of us was sure if live chickens were allowed to travel on British trains, so he tucked the bird up safely in a cat-carrying box that he veiled in some colorful drapes (luckily she was unperturbed by any lingering traces of cat scent, and refrained from squawking during the journey).

Ian and the bird arrived at my home in a taxi after dark. She was a beautiful creature, clean and plump, with a coat of snow-white feathers. There was a grace about her, and she looked me steadily in the eye. We tried to make her feel at home, bedding her down on some old copies of the *China Daily* and giving her a last supper of corn and water. I chatted and clucked to her, feeling guilty at my own perfidy. (There are all kinds of crimes against the laws of hospitality, but surely the worst thing you can do to a houseguest is murder her?) Whatever her suspicions, she settled down quietly for the night, with just the occasional cluck or purr-like trill as she nested.

In the course of many years exploring China, I have seen plenty of carnage in the markets. When I lived in Chengdu, the poultry stalls were a mess of blood and feathers. Although bird-flu scares have largely driven live poultry stalls out of the cities, fish and eels are still commonly killed and cleaned to order. As a cook, I have been confronted from time to time by slaughter and gore. I have killed and gutted fish, crabs, and eels. I've plucked and gutted pheasants ever since, as a teenager besotted with the fundamentals of cookery, I persuaded my mother to buy me a brace in feather. But I had never killed a chicken.

I do believe that anyone who eats meat should be prepared to face up to what this means, and I'm not particularly squeamish.

At the same time, however, I couldn't help but remember a conversation I'd had with an American friend only weeks before about his own conversion to vegetarianism. He'd been out hunting with his father on a bitterly cold winter's day, and they had killed one of a pair of geese by the side of a frozen lake. The goose's mate had circled over them for what seemed to him like an age, honking in distress or anger. Even when they had loaded the dead fowl into the car and driven off, its widowed spouse had followed their car, circling overhead and honking. "And I couldn't get it out of my head," he said, "that constant honking."

Ian and I rose early the next morning. It was a cold November day. We let the bird walk around for a while, and then we took it outside to do the necessary deed. Self-consciously, and a little furtively, we killed it in my front yard, to the amazement of a couple of passersby who happened to glance over the wall. Following Chinese procedure, I caught most of the blood in a glass vessel that already held a little water, a sprinkling of salt, and a dash of oil. I gave the mixture a stir, and then took it upstairs to set it in a bain-marie. I dunked the bird into a potful of hot water to loosen its plumes. And then I went back outside and sat on the blood-spattered

step to strip off the feathers, which fell away easily into my hands.

Upstairs in my apartment, I cut the bird open and pulled out the warm, glistening mass of viscera. I sorted out the innards, carefully discarding the greenish sac of bile, salvaging the liver, the just-stilled heart, and the purplish gizzard with its frondy patterns of white. In the sink, I slit open the intestines with a scissor blade and rinsed them clean, rubbing them with salt and Shaoxing wine. And then I cut off the head and feet (trimming away the toenails), and jointed and boned the bird. I set the carcass to simmer in a potful of water, with purifying ginger, scallion, and Shaoxing wine. By now I had all the parts required for the recipes, and the real prep could begin.

Like many Chinese cookbooks, my written source for the chicken extravaganza was vague about quantities, so I had to make them up. And I couldn't resist tweaking a few of the recipes to suit my Sichuanese tastes. While Chef Wang suggested dressing the chicken's wings, head, and feet with soy sauce, vinegar, sugar, and sesame oil, I added some Sichuanese chili oil and a pinch of Sichuan pepper. His proposed stir-fry of cubed chicken thigh with red pepper seemed like an open invitation for a bit of Sichuanese heat and vivacity, so I also prepared some pickled chili paste and garlic. And because I couldn't find Chef Wang's Jiangsu pickled cucumber and ginger in London, I opted instead for Sichuanese preserved mustard tuber (*zha cai*), for its equally delectable salty-sour crispness. I also chose to substitute vegetable oil for lard, reckoning that it would be impossible for me to serve all the dishes simultaneously, and wanting to avoid the unattractive congealment of cooling lard.

It's a cliché that Chinese cooking is all about the prep, but it's also often the truth. The slicing and marinating for my nine dishes took several hours. My work was complicated by the fact that I had broken my right wrist only six weeks before and was

still recovering. I could, apparently, bone and joint a chicken, but when it came to the laborious pummeling of the breast into a smooth paste, a skill I had learned as a apprentice chef in Sichuan, my wrist protested and I had to ask Ian to put down his camera and take up a pair of cleavers, while I looked bossily over his shoulder, insisting that he pick out every wisp of tendon.

By the time I was ready to actually cook, the kitchen table and counters were covered in a multitude of tiny bowls and dishes. There were bowls of sliced innards, puréed breast in two different formations, chunks of drumstick, slivered breast, cubed thigh, boiled extremities, sauces, batters, finely chopped scallion and ginger, sliced garlic, ham, bamboo shoots and mushrooms, chopped blanched spinach, and other bits and pieces. The stock, still simmering away, had begun to perfume the kitchen with its beguiling richness, and my recipe note cards were spattered with soy sauce and oil.

After that, everything happened very fast. I dressed the boiled head, feet, and wings in my Sichuanese dressing to make the dish charmingly named *fei jiao*

tiao—"fly-squawk-jump." I cloaked the drumstick pieces in a golden egg-yolk batter and deep-fried them into chicken nuggets redolent with the aromas of scallion and Sichuan pepper. I whipped up the two separate thigh stir-fries, velveting the meat in mildly hot oil and then wokking it more fiercely with the appropriate seasonings, first with pickled chilies, ginger, scallion, and garlic; and second, unusually, with cubes of crisp apple. I stir-fried the finely slivered breast with Sichuanese preserved vegetable. The little odds and ends of offal—the crisp gizzard, sleek liver, and bouncy heart—were thinly sliced and *bao* (stir-fried at a high temperature), with slices of water chestnut for a pleasing crunch.

Trickiest were the puréed chicken breast concoctions. The first, "snowflake chicken," involved pouring a whipped breast emulsion into poaching oil, hot enough to cook it gently while preserving its custardy mouthfeel, and then swiftly stir-frying the cloudlike morsels with bamboo shoot and mushroom. The second was a *geng*, or thick soup, of diluted breast thickened with starch, ornamented with a little reserved

breast soup colored green by spinach and drizzled onto the surface in the classic Taiji design, depicting the eternal ebb and flow of *yin* and *yang*. Finally, I made a soothing broth by adding the jellied blood and ribbony intestines, along with sliced mushroom and bamboo shoot, to that sumptuous chicken stock.

We laid all the dishes out on a dark background, and I felt a flush of pride and satisfaction. I could hardly believe I had managed to follow in Chef Wang Suhua's footsteps, slaughtering the bird on the doorstep without being arrested, washing my first chicken intestines, testing and documenting nine new recipes that had all turned out fine. There were still a few white feathers on the kitchen floor, and the whole room was spattered with oil and littered with a miscellany of empty bowls and seasonings. The cat box yawned emptily in the hallway, and a few spots of blood remained outside at the scene of the crime. But there, amid the devastation, those nine little dishes sat serenely in their military formation, a testament to the transformative magic of Chinese cuisine.

One Chicken Eaten in Nine Ways

To make the full set of recipes, you will need a live chicken, around four and a half pounds in weight, and a whole day ahead of you (we killed the chicken at around ten a.m., and I finished cooking at about four p.m.). I'm still not quite sure of the best order to attack the recipes: it will be fantastically complicated whichever way you tackle them! The most important thing is to set the stock to simmer as soon as possible, and then to do all your prep before you attempt to actually cook the dishes.

The chicken feast serves about four people generously, perhaps six in a pinch, with plain steamed rice.

KILLING, CLEANING, AND JOINTING YOUR BIRD

You can find detailed instructions and photographs explaining how to kill, pluck, clean, and joint your bird on various websites (for example: the blog *BackYard Chickens*). Do check out local laws and regulations on humane slaughter.

To kill a chicken for the following recipes, you will need to collect the fresh blood, which means slitting the bird's throat—preferably after first stunning it or wringing its neck. To process the blood in the Chinese way, first place a scant ½ cup cold water, ¼ teaspoon salt, and ½ teaspoon vegetable oil in a heat-proof vessel large enough to catch the blood; drain the fresh blood directly into this vessel and immediately mix everything together very well. Leave the blood mixture for a few minutes—it will congeal. Then boil the blood for several minutes in a bain–marie, until it

has set to a dark, purplish jelly. Leave to cool before slicing.

When you gut the chicken, retain the liver, heart, gizzard, and intestines. Cut the gizzard in half; remove and discard the partially digested grain in the center, along with the lining that encloses it. Slice open the intestines: I found the easiest way to do this was to insert a sharp scissor blade in one end and then run it along the length of the tube, slitting it open. Rinse the intestines very thoroughly under the cold tap, and then place in a bowl. Add ½ teaspoon salt and rub it in; then rinse again. Do the same with another ½ teaspoon salt and a splash of Shaoxing wine. When the intestines are completely clean and the rinse water is clear, they are ready for cooking.

After jointing the chicken, debone the

thighs. Then debone the drumsticks and the upper parts of the wings. Save all the bones for the stock, and retain the head, feet, and the rest of the wings. You should end up with the following parts:

1 carcass
2 boneless breasts
2 boneless thighs
2 boneless drumsticks
2 boneless upper wing joints
2 lower wing joints
2 feet
1 head
1 neck
1 heart
1 liver
1 gizzard
intestines
congealed blood jelly

Recipes are based on those in *Jiangsu Fengwei Caidian*, a 1989 textbook by Chen Zhongming, produced by the Chinese Cooking Department of the Jiangsu Commercial Training College.

NOW YOU ARE

READY TO COOK!

Chicken Stock

MAKES 6 CUPS

1 2" piece ginger, with the skin on
2 scallions, white parts only
1 chicken carcass with the leg bones,
    wing bones, and neck
1 T Shaoxing wine

1. Smack the ginger and scallion whites with the side of a cleaver blade to loosen their fibers. Bring a large potful of water to boil over a high flame. Add the chicken carcass and boil 2–3 minutes, allowing any impurities to rise to the surface.

2. Tip the carcass into a colander and rinse thoroughly under the cold tap, discarding the blanching water. Then return the carcass to the pot, cover with fresh water, and bring to boil over a high flame. Skim the impurities from the surface if necessary.

3. Add the ginger, scallions, and Shaoxing wine. Lower the heat and simmer while you prepare the other ingredients.

DISH 1:

Chinese Chicken Nuggets
(zha ji kuai, 炸鸡块)
MAKES 4 SERVINGS

¼ t Sichuan pepper
2 boneless drumsticks
2 boneless upper wing joints
1 scallion, white part only
2 t light soy sauce
1 t Shaoxing wine
¼ t fine-grained salt
2 egg yolks
3 T potato starch or cornstarch
2¼ C neutral oil for deep-frying,
    plus more as needed
½ t sesame oil

1. Soak the peppercorns for a minute or two in hot water from a kettle. Cut the chicken as evenly as possible into ¾-inch chunks. Place the scallion on a board and finely chop. Add the drained peppercorns and continue chopping until you have a pepper-fragrant scallion mix. Add this to the chicken chunks along with the soy sauce, Shaoxing wine, and salt and mix well to combine. Set aside.

2. When you are ready to cook the nuggets, mix the egg yolks and starch together to form a batter. Add the chicken pieces and mix to coat evenly.

3. Heat the oil in a seasoned wok over a high flame to 330°F. Drop the chicken pieces individually into the hot oil, using chopsticks to keep them separate. When the chicken is cooked through after 2–3 minutes (cut open one piece to make sure), remove the pieces from the wok with a slotted spoon.

4. Let the oil temperature rise to 430°F. Return the nuggets to the wok and fry until golden. Drain well and serve with a sprinkling of sesame oil.

DISH 2:

Fly-Squawk-Jump

(*fei jiao tiao*, 飞叫跳)

MAKES 4 SERVINGS

2 chicken feet
1 chicken head
2 lower wing joints
+ hot **Chicken Stock** (enough to immerse the chicken bits)
2½ T light soy sauce
½ t sugar
½ t Chinkiang vinegar
1 T cold **Chicken Stock**
¼ t sesame oil
1 T chili oil
+ a pinch ground roasted Sichuan pepper
+ cilantro sprigs, for garnish

1. Trim the toenails from the feet. Bring a pot of water to a boil, add the chicken parts, and blanch for 1–2 minutes. Remove the chicken and rinse well under the cold tap, discarding the water.

2. In a large pot, bring the hot Chicken Stock to a boil. Add the chicken parts and simmer for about 10 minutes. Remove, drain, and leave to cool.

3. Combine the light soy sauce, sugar, vinegar, cold Chicken Stock, sesame oil, chili oil, and Sichuan pepper in a small bowl.

4. To serve, arrange the chicken parts in a bowl, pour the sauce over the top, and garnish with a sprig of cilantro.

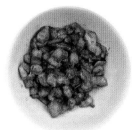

DISH 3:

Exploded Offal with Water Chestnuts

(*bao zhun gan xin*, 爆肫肝心)

MAKES 4 SERVINGS

1 chicken gizzard
1 chicken liver
1 chicken heart
⅛ t fine-grained salt
1 t Shaoxing wine
¾ t potato starch
1 t cold water
1 T + ½ t neutral oil
¼ C peeled water chestnuts
+ Sauce
1 t finely chopped ginger
2 garlic cloves sliced
1 t finely chopped scallion
+ a pinch white pepper

SAUCE

¼ t potato starch
½ t sugar
½ t Chinkiang vinegar
1½ t light soy sauce
¼ t dark soy sauce
1 T cold **Chicken Stock**
¼ t sesame oil

1. Cut the gizzard, liver, and heart into very thin slices. Combine the salt, Shaoxing wine, potato starch, and cold water and mix well. Then stir in ½ teaspoon of the neutral oil and add the offal slices. Cut the water chestnuts into very thin slices and set aside.

2. Combine the Sauce ingredients in a small bowl. Set aside.

3. When you are ready to cook, heat a seasoned wok over a high flame. Add 1 tablespoon of neutral oil. When hot, add the offal with the ginger, garlic, and scallion and stir-fry briefly to separate the pieces of meat. When the offal is just cooked, stir in the water chestnuts. Give the Sauce a stir and add to the wok; mix well to combine. When the Sauce has thickened, turn onto a serving dish and sprinkle with a pinch of white pepper.

DISH 4:

Sichuanese Stir-Fried Chicken Cubes

(*la zi ji ding*, 辣子鸡丁)

MAKES 4 SERVINGS

2 boneless chicken thighs

1 t fine-grained salt

2 t Shaoxing wine

2 t potato starch

1 T egg white

1 C neutral oil

½ sweet red pepper

+ Sauce

½ **t** Sichuanese pickled
  chili paste or *sambal oelek*

1 t finely chopped ginger

1 t finely chopped scallion,
  plus 1 t finely chopped
  scallion greens, for garnish

1 garlic clove, sliced

SAUCE

¾ **t** potato starch

½ **t** sugar

1 t light soy sauce

1 T cold **Chicken Stock**

¼ **t** sesame oil

1. Cut the chicken thighs into ¾-inch cubes. In a medium bowl, combine the salt, 1 teaspoon of the Shaoxing wine, the potato starch, and egg white. Mix well. Stir in 1 teaspoon of the neutral oil and then the thighs. Divide the chicken thighs into two equal portions, retaining one for use in the **Velveted Chicken Cubes with Apple**.

2. Slice the red pepper into cubes a little smaller than the chicken cubes and set aside.

3. Combine the Sauce ingredients in a small bowl. Set aside.

4. When you are ready to cook, heat the remaining oil in a seasoned wok to 290°F. Add one of the portions of marinated chicken thighs and stir rapidly to separate the pieces. When the pieces have become pale, pour the chicken and

oil through a metal sieve into a heatproof container to catch the oil.

5. Return the wok to a high flame with 1 tablespoon of the oil. Add the chili paste or sambal oelek, ginger, scallion, and garlic and stir-fry very briefly, until sizzling. Add the chicken and red pepper and stir to combine.

6. Pour the remaining teaspoon of Shaoxing wine around the edges of the wok and let it sizzle. When everything is hot and the chicken just cooked through, give the Sauce a stir and add to the wok. Stir as the Sauce thickens, then serve with the scallion garnish.

Velveted Chicken Cubes with Apple

(ping guo liu ji ding, 苹果熘鸡丁)

MAKES 4 SERVINGS

¼ **t** sugar

½ **t** potato starch

½ **t** light soy sauce

½ **t** Chinkiang vinegar

1 T cold **Chicken Stock**

¼ **t** sesame oil

1 C neutral oil

+ reserved portion of marinated chicken thighs from the **Sichuanese Stir-Fried Chicken Cubes**

1 garlic clove, sliced

½ medium crisp apple, peeled, cored, and cut into ¾-inch cubes

2 t Shaoxing wine

1. In a small bowl, whisk together the sugar, potato starch, soy sauce, vinegar, Chicken Stock, and sesame oil and set aside.

2. Heat the neutral oil in a seasoned wok to 290°F. Give the chicken pieces a stir to loosen and carefully add to the hot oil, stirring to separate. When the pieces have become pale, pour the chicken and oil through a metal sieve into a heatproof container to catch the oil.

3. Return the wok to a high flame with 1 tablespoon of the oil and the sliced garlic. Stir-fry briefly until the garlic sizzles, then add the apple and chicken and stir-fry until hot and sizzling. Pour the Shaoxing wine around the edges of the wok, then give the sauce mixture a stir and add to the wok. Stir as the sauce thickens, then serve.

Stir-Fried Chicken Slivers
with Sichuanese Preserved Vegetable
(*zha cai ji si*, 榨菜鸡丝)
MAKES 4 SERVINGS

1 boneless chicken breast

¼ t fine-grained salt

1 T Shaoxing wine

4 t potato starch

3 T cold water

1 C neutral oil

¼ C Sichuanese preserved
    mustard tuber (*zha cai*)

1. Cut the chicken breast into very thin slices and then into very thin slivers, as thin as possible along the grain of the meat.

2. Combine the salt, 2 teaspoons of Shaoxing wine, 2 teaspoons potato starch, and 1 tablespoon of the cold water in a medium bowl and mix well to combine. Stir in 1 teaspoon of the neutral oil, then the chicken.

3. Cut the preserved vegetable into very thin slices and then slivers, to match the chicken. Set aside.

4. Heat the remaining oil in a seasoned wok over a high flame to 250°F. Add the chicken slivers and stir rapidly to separate. As soon as they change color, pour the chicken and oil through a metal sieve into a heatproof container to catch the oil.

5. Return the wok to a high flame with 1 tablespoon of the oil. Add the preserved vegetable slivers and stir-fry briefly until sizzling. Return the chicken slivers to the wok and stir-fry until piping hot. Sizzle the remaining teaspoon of Shaoxing wine around the edges of the wok.

6. In a small bowl, combine the remaining 2 teaspoons of potato starch with 2 tablespoons of cold water. Give the mixture a stir and pour into the center of the wok, stirring as it thickens. Serve.

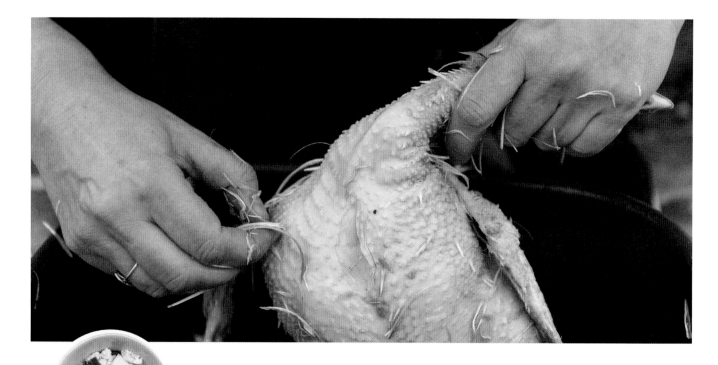

DISH 7:

Snowflake Chicken
(*xue hua ji pian*, 雪花鸡片)
MAKES 4 SERVINGS

1 boneless chicken breast

1 2" piece ginger, with skin on

2 scallions, white parts only

1 C cold water

¾ t fine-grained salt

1 T potato starch

2 T egg white

2 dried shiitake mushrooms, soaked for at least 30 minutes in hot water

2 T winter bamboo shoots (canned is fine)

1 C neutral oil

2 t Shaoxing wine

¾ t potato starch mixed with 2 T cold water

+ slices of cooked ham, for garnish

+ cilantro leaves, for garnish

1. Place the chicken breast on a wooden board and pummel it with the blunt back of a cleaver blade (or, better, the blunt backs of a pair of cleavers). Keep "chopping" the meat, backward and forward, turning it over and around on the board, until it is reduced to a smooth paste. Then hold the cleaver blade at a close angle to the board and spread the paste out—this will allow you to pick out any white wisps of tendon whole, allowing for a perfectly smooth paste. Place the paste in a bowl.

2. Smack the ginger and scallion whites with the flat side of the cleaver blade to loosen them, then place in a bowl and add the cold water. Add the salt to the chicken paste and mix well. Then stir in the potato starch and egg white, mixing thoroughly. Strain the ginger-scallion water, discarding the solids. Stir the chicken paste in one direction (it's easiest to do this with your hand), gradually adding the strained ginger-scallion water until it has all been incorporated. Divide the paste into two equal portions, retaining one for the **Taiji Chicken Soup**.

3. Cut the soaked shiitakes and bamboo shoots into thin slices. Drop the bamboo shoots into a little boiling water and blanch for a minute or so to refresh them; drain.

4. When you are ready to cook, heat the oil in a seasoned wok over a high flame to 250°F. Pour in one portion of the chicken paste and stir gently with the ladle. When the paste has floated to the surface in cloudlike pieces, pour the chicken and oil through a metal sieve into a heatproof container to catch the oil.

5. Return the wok to a high flame with 1 tablespoon of the oil. Add the sliced shiitakes and bamboo shoots and stir-fry until piping hot. Return the chicken to the wok, and pour the Shaoxing wine around the edges. Give the starch mixture a stir and pour it into the center of the wok, stirring as it thickens. Turn everything onto a serving dish and garnish with the sliced ham and cilantro leaves.

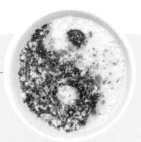

DISH 8:

Taiji Chicken Soup
(*tai ji ji geng*, 太极鸡羹)
MAKES 4 SERVINGS

2 handfuls baby spinach

¼ t fine-grained salt

1½ C Chicken Stock

+ reserved portion of chicken-breast paste from **Snowflake Chicken**

1 t neutral oil (or lard)

2 T potato starch mixed with ¼ C cold water

2 t very finely chopped cooked ham, for garnish

SPECIAL EQUIPMENT

+ a clean, flexible piece of plastic to make the Taiji shape (I cut a strip from a plastic document folder)

1. Place the baby spinach in a sieve and pour a kettleful of boiling water over to wilt it. Refresh the spinach immediately under cold tap water. When completely cool, squeeze out as much water as possible and chop as finely as possible. Set aside.

2. Add the salt and the Chicken Stock to the chicken paste and mix well to combine. Heat the chicken paste with the oil in a seasoned wok over a high flame, stirring constantly. When it has come to a boil, give the starch mixture a stir and add it, in stages, until the liquid has a thick consistency. Pour most of the liquid into a serving bowl, leaving about 2 tablespoons in the wok.

3. Add the chopped spinach to the remaining liquid and mix well to incorporate.

4. Bend your piece of plastic into a yin-yang curve and place it in the serving bowl so its bottom edge is dipped into the soup. Carefully spoon the green chicken soup onto one side of the plastic to create the correct shape. Carefully remove the plastic. Then, use a teaspoon to remove a tiny amount of soup from the white side and drop it into the correct place on the green side, and vice versa. Garnish with a little chopped ham and serve.

DISH 9:
Chicken Blood and Intestine Soup
(*ji za tang*, 鸡杂汤)
MAKES 4 SERVINGS

+ congealed blood jelly
+ cleaned chicken intestines
3 dried shiitake mushrooms, soaked for at least 30 minutes in hot water
2 T winter bamboo shoots (canned is fine)
1 T neutral oil
1 t finely chopped ginger
1 t finely chopped scallion
2¼ C Chicken Stock
2 t Shaoxing wine

+ fine-grained salt
+ a pinch white pepper
1 cilantro sprig, for garnish

1. Cut the jellied chicken blood into ⅛-inch slices (you will only need about half of it). Cut the intestines into 1¾-inch lengths. Thinly slice the soaked mushrooms and bamboo shoots. Blanch the bamboo slices in boiling water for a minute or so to refresh.

2. Heat the oil in a seasoned wok over a high flame. Add the ginger and scallions and stir-fry very briefly, until they sizzle. Add the Chicken Stock and bring to a boil. Add the blood, mushrooms, and bamboo shoots and return the mixture to a boil. Add the Shaoxing wine and salt to taste.

3. Finally, add the intestines to the wok and return to a boil. Pour into a serving dish. Sprinkle with white pepper and garnish with cilantro to serve. **LP**

Assisting the amazing
since 1886

SPICE UP YOUR MENU

Made from triple-fermented wheat for intense umami flavor, *Maggi*® Spicy Seasoning adds flavor complexity with the unique heat of Sichuan peppers. Bring out the flavor in dishes across cuisines in everything from sauces and dips to marinades and beverages.

Request your free sample at nestleprofessional.com/maggi or call 1-800-288-8682

3

Chicken — Soup

By Brette Warshaw   *Photographs by Gabriele Stabile* ——————

Dishes

Is there anything more clichéd than chicken soup?

That is a rhetorical question. The answer is no, and I won't drag you through some extended joke where I invoke the universality of the dish by comparing it to the sprawling list of titles in the *Chicken Soup for the Soul* series. (Even though as a woman in publishing, I am *fascinated* by how far they've taken that brand and would love to know how *Chicken Soup for the Horse Lover's Soul* did well enough to publish a sequel.)

But this column isn't about publishing or horses or clichés: it's about cooking. And for this issue's Three Dishes, we're examining three iterations of the world's most anodyne dish from three New York restaurants.

Take one is pure, steaming chicken juice to be sipped from a mug. It's Marco Canora's recipe for bone broth, a foodstuff that was hot like Icarus in 2014 but remains delicious today, made at home or picked up from either of the two outposts of Brodo.

Take two is the food of my people: a dead-simple matzo ball soup, from Katz's Delicatessen, a paragon of delis on the Lower East Side. Jake Dell, who runs Katz's today, gives us a no-nonsense classic run-through of the recipe, the sort of simmer-it-in-a-pot-and-let-God-sort-it-out attitude that usually gets ascribed to grandmotherly cooking.

The third spin on chicken soup is a loads-of-work curry called *khao soi* from Thailand, courtesy of Ann Redding and Matt Danzer of Uncle Boons in Nolita. Khao soi, if you don't know it, is a soupy stew of chicken, coconut milk, egg noodles, and lots of herbs and spices, topped with garnishes like shallots, lime, pickled mustard greens, and more of those egg noodles fried into a crispy tangle. It is unexpectedly complex compared to the simplicity of the first two soups, but eating it scratches that same, clichéd comfort itch and shows the range and diversity of forms that chicken soup can take.

— *Brette Warshaw*

Brodo

Chicken Brodo

When I first opened Brodo, everyone wanted to obsess about the nomenclature. *What's bone broth? Is it broth or is it stock?*

In the kitchens I came up in, there was a distinction between stock and broth: stock is typically made with more bone, and broth is made with more meat. French techniques are really built around stock, where you start with bones and knuckles—veal knuckles in particular, because those young cows have a lot of collagen in their bones. Collagen allows you to reduce the stock more, and the viscosity of the resulting liquid makes it the perfect vehicle for many French reductions and sauces.

When you use more meat than bones, you get a lighter, clearer, more flavorful broth, as opposed to a darker, more gelatinous stock. It doesn't get the same rich viscosity, but it tends to have more flavor. If you look at the Italian repertoire, you see a lot of simple soups—escarole soup, *tortellini en brodo, stracciatella*—built on a really good broth.

But at the end of the day, it doesn't matter what you call it. That debate can get tired. You can call it broth; you can call it stock; you can call it bone broth. It's transformative magic.

I use necks, backs, and feet. The feet have a lot of cartilage, and the cartilage is what breaks down into gelatin. And what's cool about the neck bone, as opposed to other bones—especially when you talk about larger animals like cows, pigs, and lambs—is that it has all of these nooks and crannies. It's very hard for a processing plant to strip all of the meat off that bone, so you end up getting both bone and meat, which is ideal for broth. A lot of people make beef broth using marrow bones, which are really easy to strip the meat off of—so you end up making a broth with only bone and fat. It's not going to yield you the umami-rich, colored, gelatinous thing that you want. Making a rich and complex broth requires a surprisingly generous ratio of bones to water; otherwise you'll end up with a watery broth that lacks depth of flavor.

And this makes some people's eyes roll, but I really believe in the functional benefits of drinking broth. There is absolutely a reason why we've been making this for thirty thousand years, and there's a reason why every culture around the globe has a broth practice. I believe it is critical to our health, that having broth in your diet throughout the year helps build a healthy gut. I am 100 percent behind the idea that without a healthy gut, you have inflammation, and chronic inflammation is the source behind the shit that is happening to our health, whether it's acne, IBS, heart problems, or arthritic problems.

More than anything, I feel like a cup of broth represents everything I want to stand for as a chef. The simplicity, depth of flavor, and satisfaction you get from broth define what I've tried to do as a chef my whole life: make sure the food feels good going in and make sure it feels good when you're done eating it, and never sacrifice the satisfaction part. A well-made cup of broth can hit all of those marks, in my mind, in such a powerful way.

—*Marco Canora*

Chicken Brodo

MAKES ABOUT 6 QUARTS

4 lbs chicken necks and backs
1 lb chicken feet
2 small yellow onions, peeled
and coarsely chopped
1 large carrot, peeled
and coarsely chopped
3 celery stalks, coarsely chopped
1½ t whole black peppercorns
3 bay leaves
+ fine sea salt

1. Heat the oven to 375°F.

2. Arrange the necks and backs in a single layer on a rimmed baking sheet. Roast until well browned, about 1 hour, flipping halfway through.

3. Place the necks, backs, and feet in an 8-quart pot. Add cold water to cover by 2–3 inches, about 5 quarts. Bring to a boil over high heat, skimming off the foamy impurities every 15–20 minutes.

4. As soon as the liquid starts boiling, reduce the heat to low and pull the pot to one side so it is partially off the burner. This allows for the liquid to circulate in the pot. Simmer for 1 hour and 30 minutes, uncovered, skimming once or twice.

5. Add the onions, carrot, celery, peppercorns, and bay leaves and push them down into the liquid. Continue to simmer for 3–5 hours, uncovered, skimming as needed and occasionally checking to make sure the bones are still fully submerged.

6. Use a slotted spoon to remove the solids and discard. Strain the broth through a fine-mesh strainer. Season with salt to taste and let cool.

7. Transfer the cooled broth to storage containers and refrigerate overnight. When the broth is chilled, spoon off any solidified fat (the broth itself will be congealed). Store the broth for up to 5 days in the refrigerator or freeze for up to 6 months. Rewarm brodo in a pot to serve.

Adapted from Brodo: A Bone Broth
Cookbook *by Marco Canora*

HOW TO SKIM

When you bring a pot of bones and water up to a boil, the bones will release what are usually called impurities. They're not particularly impure, they're really just food particles and fat. If you leave them in the stock, though, they will eventually disperse into the broth and give it a cloudy, grayish color. So to get a clear, pretty broth that looks as good as it tastes, that's the stuff you want to get rid of. Here are some thoughts about skimmery from Marco Canora:

— When you're adding water to the pot, make sure it's a couple of inches over the level of the bones. Those couple of inches aren't part of a magical ratio; it's so you can fit your ladle in there. If you don't leave enough headspace, your ladle won't fit, and you won't be able to skim properly.

— When it's time to skim, slowly lower the ladle into the pot. As soon as the edge of it breaks the surface tension on the top of the water level, freeze. Don't move the ladle all around the top of the pot; you're going to scoop up too much of the good stuff. The scum should flow right in.

— It's easy to underestimate the amount of time it will take to bring the bones and water to a boil. The scum will continue to rise to the top in the first hour or two; repeat the above process as needed until there's no more scum to skim.

Katz's

Matzo Ball Soup

We start the soup at Katz's by roasting chickens; we pick off the meat and use it for our chicken salad and use what remains in our chicken broth. The same broth is used for the matzo ball soup and the chicken noodle soup.

Matzo balls are pretty straightforward: you take a shit ton of eggs, beat them with some matzo meal, and let it sit. Add some seltzer to fluff it up, or you can add some baking powder. They're really a way to take something that tastes like cardboard—matzo is the worst—and make it taste good. Mix some matzo with some eggs and fat, and you're good to go. It's really not that complicated.

The soup here at Katz's is actually the product of dueling grandmothers: the Katz family had a contest to see which grandma had the best recipe. You're eating the winning grandma's soup today.

I'm the fifth generation now. My grandfather was partners with the original Katz family. I grew up here in this business, and I know how many New Yorkers and people all over the country have a strong connection to this place.

—*Jake Dell*

Delicatessen

Matzo Ball Soup

MAKES 6 SERVINGS

1 leftover carcass from a roast chicken, broken in half, or 1½ lbs leftover cooked chicken bones and scraps
1 small white onion, peeled and chopped
2 celery stalks, chopped
2 small carrots, peeled and chopped
+ kosher salt
+ freshly ground black pepper
+ Matzo Balls, warmed
+ chopped dill, for garnish

1. Combine the chicken carcass, onion, half the celery, and half the carrots in a large pot. Cover with water, about 8 cups, and bring to a boil over high heat, skimming any impurities from the surface around every 5 minutes.

2. As soon as the liquid starts boiling, reduce the heat to maintain a gentle simmer and continue cooking until the broth is light brown and slightly reduced, about 2 hours.

3. Using tongs, lift the chicken bones from the broth and discard. Pour the broth through a fine-mesh strainer into a medium saucepan and season with salt and pepper. Bring to a gentle simmer, then add the remaining celery and carrots and cook until the vegetables are tender, 8–10 minutes.

4. Divide the Matzo Balls among 6 serving bowls and ladle the broth and vegetables over the top. Garnish with dill and serve immediately.

Matzo Balls

MAKES 6 BALLS

1½ C matzo meal
3 T seltzer
2 T finely chopped dill
1½ T schmaltz
1½ t kosher salt, plus more as needed
½ t freshly ground black pepper
7 large eggs

1. In a large bowl, beat together all of the ingredients until thoroughly combined; the mixture will be loose at first but will thicken upon resting. Cover and hold in the refrigerator at least 2 hours or overnight.

2. Bring a large saucepan of salted water to a boil over high heat.

3. Lightly wet your hands, then roll the batter into 6 balls. Drop the balls into the boiling water. Once they begin to float, after 1 minute, gently stir and continue to boil until they swell to the size of softballs, about 15 minutes more. Carefully remove the matzo balls with a slotted spoon and transfer to a serving bowl if eating right away. If storing for later, transfer the matzo balls to a container and cover with water. Matzo balls will keep in the refrigerator for 5 days.

Uncle

Khao Soi

ANN REDDING: Khao soi is a specialty of the Chiang Mai region; it's the dish that the area is known for. Chiang Mai is a lot cooler than Bangkok, so the spices and the warm, savory flavors really suit the dish.

Our khao soi is actually one of the few dishes on our menu that we didn't play with that much—it's such a perfect dish the way it is, and it's so comforting that we wanted to leave it mostly alone. The chopped cilantro in the egg noodles, though—that isn't traditional. We add that for a little extra punch. Matt first wanted to do a pappardelle with a cilantro inlay—whole leaves of cilantro perfectly rolled into the dough—but it got to be a bit much.

MATT DANZER: It used to take the guys, like, six hours to make the pasta dough. So I finally said, *Okay, fine, you can chop the cilantro.*

We grind up our harder items, like spices, then grind the spices and vegetables down to a paste. Traditionally, they say you're supposed to sweat the paste until you stick your head over the pot and it makes you sneeze. Then we add all of the other liquids: we braise chicken legs in the paste mixed with chicken stock and coconut milk and then let it rest overnight. Like many braises, it's better the next day.

Boons

Khao Soi

MAKES 4 SERVINGS

1 *pandan* leaf
4 skinless chicken drumsticks
4 skinless chicken thighs
+ **Khao Soi Sauce**
+ kosher salt
+ **Cilantro Egg Noodles**
+ **Pickled Shallots**, pickled mustard greens (you can find these at most Asian grocery stores), chopped scallions, cilantro sprigs, and **Fried Cilantro Egg Noodles**, for garnish
+ lime wedges and chili sauce, for serving

1. Heat the oven to 325°F.

2. Place the pandan leaf, drumsticks, and thighs in a large roasting pan. Pour the Khao Soi Sauce over the top and cover with foil. Braise until very tender, around 1½–2 hours.

3. Using tongs, transfer the thighs to a cutting board and let cool for 5 minutes. Pick the thigh meat off the bones, then return the picked meat to the sauce; leave the drumsticks intact. If not serving right away, cover the roasting pan and refrigerate overnight (it's better the next day). Bring the sauce and meat to a simmer for 5 minutes before serving.

4. When you're almost ready to serve, bring a large pot of salted water to a boil. Drop in the Cilantro Egg Noodles and cook until al dente, about 3 minutes. Drain the noodles and divide them among 4 large serving bowls.

5. Remove the chicken from the sauce and place on top of the noodles, dividing the drumsticks and thigh meat evenly among the bowls. Ladle the sauce over top of the chicken, then garnish with the Pickled Shallots, pickled mustard greens, scallions, cilantro, and a large handful of the Fried Cilantro Egg Noodles (you will have some fried noodles leftover). Serve immediately with lime wedges and chili sauce on the side.

Khao Soi Sauce

MAKES 8 CUPS

6 C full-fat coconut milk
⅔ C Khao Soi Paste
1½ C chicken stock, homemade or store bought
½ C + 1 T fish sauce
3 T dark soy sauce
2 T finely chopped palm sugar or packed light brown sugar
+ kosher salt, to taste

1. Skim the thick coconut cream off the top of the coconut milk, transfer it to a large saucepan, and heat over medium-high heat. Simmer until it begins to thicken and separate, about 5 minutes. Add the Khao Soi Paste and cook, stirring, until fragrant, about 2 minutes.

2. Add the coconut milk, chicken stock, fish sauce, dark soy sauce, and palm sugar and bring to a boil. Remove from the heat and season with salt to taste. Transfer the sauce to a container, if not using right away, and store in the refrigerator for up to 1 week.

Khao Soi Paste

MAKES 1 HEAPING CUP

This will more than what you need for the recipe; what's left over is good stirred into scrambled eggs, tossed into rice dishes, sautéed with any simple protein, or in another round of Khao Soi. It will keep in the refrigerator for up to 1 week, or you can freeze it for future use.

12 dried *árbol* chilies, stemmed
6–8 large shallots (1 lb), sliced
12 garlic cloves, sliced
1 3" piece fresh ginger, peeled and sliced
1 3" piece fresh turmeric, peeled and sliced
2 T olive oil
1½ T whole coriander seeds
3 brown (or black) cardamom pods
½ C finely chopped cilantro stems
1 t kosher salt

1. Heat the oven to 425°F.

2. In a large bowl, soak the chilies in 1 cup boiling water for 10 minutes. Drain and pat them dry, then stir in the shallots, garlic, ginger, turmeric, and olive oil. Toss until combined, then spread on a large, rimmed baking sheet and roast, stirring once halfway through, until charred and soft, 25–30 minutes. Let cool.

3. Meanwhile, heat the coriander seeds and cardamom pods in a small skillet over high heat until toasted and fragrant, about 2 minutes. Pick out the cardamom pods and pour the coriander seeds into a spice grinder or mortar and pestle. Crack open the cardamom pods and remove the seeds inside. Discard the pods and transfer the seeds to the spice grinder. Process the spices until finely ground.

3. In a food processor, combine the roasted aromatics with the ground spices, cilantro, and salt and process until smooth. Transfer the paste to a container, cover, and refrigerate until ready to use, up to 1 week.

Cilantro Egg Noodles

MAKES 4 SERVINGS

3 T olive oil
3 large eggs
3 large egg yolks
6 T water
4 C all-purpose flour, plus more for sprinkling
1 T kosher salt, plus more as needed
½ C finely chopped cilantro leaves
+ cornstarch, for dusting
+ neutral oil, for frying

1. In a medium bowl, lightly beat together the olive oil, eggs, egg yolks, and water lightly to combine.

2. In a large bowl, combine the flour and salt. Pile onto a large, flat work surface and make a well in the center.

3. Pour the egg mixture into the center of the well. Working slowly, combine the flour into the egg, mixing together to form a dough. Sprinkle the work surface with more flour and knead until smooth. Cover with plastic wrap and refrigerate for 1 hour.

4. Divide the dough into quarters. Pass three of the dough quarters through a pasta machine on the second-to-last setting; these will be your noodles for the soup. Cut the pasta sheets crosswise in half, then cut the sheets lengthwise into ⅓-inch-wide noodles. Dust the noodles with cornstarch, transfer to a baking sheet, and refrigerate until ready to use.

5. Run the remaining quarter of dough through the pasta machine on the second-to-last setting; these will be for your Fried Cilantro Egg Noodles. Cut the pasta sheet crosswise into thirds, then cut the sheets lengthwise into ⅓-inch-wide noodles. Dust the noodles with cornstarch and refrigerate until ready to use.

6. To make the Fried Cilantro Egg Noodles: Heat a large pot of oil to 350°F. Working in batches, fry the reserved noodles until golden and crispy, about 1 minute. Drain on paper towels and hold at room temperature until ready to use.

Pickled Shallots

MAKES 1½ CUPS

½ C red wine vinegar
½ C sugar
½ t kosher salt
4 large shallots (8 oz), cut into ⅛-inch-thick slices

Combine all of the ingredients in a large container and cover with 1 cup of boiling water. Stir until the sugar and salt are dissolved. Cover and let sit in the refrigerator for at least 24 hours. **LP**

RICHT

Boneless

WITH DANIEL ROSE

Chicken

Photographs by Gabriele Stabile

A galantine is a chicken that is boned out, stuffed, rolled into a tidy log, and served like revenge: cold. (It's called a *ballotine* when it's served hot; you've gotta love classic French nomenclature.) It's a particularly economical way to eat the entire bird, but it's the diametric opposite of throwing the whole thing in the oven and roasting it.

Galantine manufacture is often a part of culinary-school curricula because it requires the special technique of deboning a whole chicken while keeping the skin intact. Trained professionals can do it in a few minutes, but that kind of deftness takes time and practice to achieve. Here, chef Daniel Rose, of Le Coucou in New York—the white-hot, fancy French restaurant of the moment, which is so close to our offices that you can actually get on our Wi-Fi there (pw: papercut128 ;))—breaks it down and rolls it up for us.

—*Joanna Sciarrino*

Daniel Rose's Chicken Galantine

with Pistachios in Red Wine Vinaigrette

MAKES 8 TO 10 SERVINGS

PREPARE THE
CHICKEN

Working with a drier bird makes the whole affair a lot easier, so it's a good idea to leave the chicken to dry out, uncovered, on a plate (or a cooling rack if you wanna go really pro) in the fridge overnight. When it's galatining time, set up your station: a nice big cutting board, a bowl for discarded parts (straight to the stockpot with those!), plastic wrap, kitchen twine, and a very sharp knife. Make sure the various things you'll be stuffing your bird with are prepared and cool and near at hand.

1 3–4 lb chicken

1 lb boneless, skinless chicken thighs

⅓ lb foie gras

2 ½ T blanched, drained, and finely
    chopped swiss chard

2 shallots, finely chopped (about ⅓ C)

+ kosher salt

+ freshly ground black pepper

⅛ lb thick-cut, good-quality smoked ham,
    cut into batons

1 C prunes soaked in ¼ C Cognac

¼ C toasted pistachio nutmeat

+ coarse sea salt

1. Dry the chicken out in the refrigerator overnight.

2. In a food processor, add the thighs, foie gras, swiss chard, shallots, salt, and pepper. Pulse until you have a coarse paste. This can be refrigerated overnight. Reserve the remaining ingredients for when you're ready to roll the galantine.

3. Debone the chicken according to the following steps.

Chicken Stuffing, or "the Farce" makes enough to fill one chicken

DR: You could put anything you want in there. It can be fancy or not fancy. This one is pretty fancy.

Jacques Pépin does this all in like three seconds.

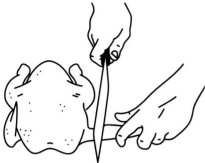

The wings don't fly on a galantine. Cut them off at the elbow joint and put them in the discard pile.

Locate the wishbone with your fingers, and make an incision along each side of the bone to release it from the breast. Pull out the wishbone with your fingers and add it to the discard bowl.

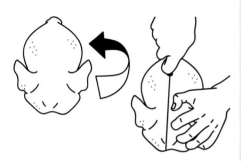

Turn the chicken onto its breast and make one long, deep incision down the center of the backbone. Pull the skin back to reveal the shoulder joint on one side of the chicken and cut through the joint with your knife to release the wing bone from the breast. Repeat on the other side, so the wings now flop from the carcass.

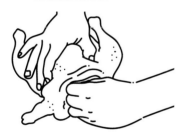

DR: You don't want to cut through the skin—you want to leave all of the skin intact except for this back part. You're actually just trying to separate using your fingers more than anything. There's not a lot of meat on the back, so we're trying to pull it all off the front.

Grab the carcass with one hand and one wing with the other and pull the wing down to tear the flesh from the carcass, stopping at the oyster, or the small nugget of flesh nestled in the back nearest the thigh. Repeat for the other wing.

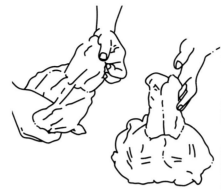

DR: The cool part about this is that you don't really have to use a knife to pry the flesh away from the cavity.

Flip the chicken over and peel the flesh down as far as it will go. Insert your first two fingers on either side of the sternum and pull down to release the flesh from the bone.

Continue to peel back the flesh on the front of the bird until the whole front of the carcass is clean. The fillets will still be attached—you'll remove them later.

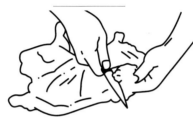

Turn the bird back over to the opened back and grab one leg. Slice into the oyster to release the flesh and pop—hyperextend—the hip, cutting through the joint with a knife to disconnect the leg from the cavity. Do the same on the other side, then pull the flesh entirely off the carcass. Remove the fillets from the carcass by running your fingers between the flesh and the bone until they peel off. Trim away any silverskin, veins, or bone from each fillet by holding one end with your fingers and scraping the flesh off with a knife. Set them aside and add the carcass to the bowl.

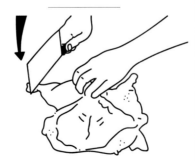

Cut the bones out of the legs: Grab one of the legs and make an L cut along the thighbone to reveal the whole bone. Using the back of a knife, crack the leg bone through the skin without tearing it, near the small end of each drumstick.

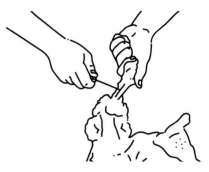

Run your knife around the end of the thigh to sever the tendons that are attached to it. Pull the thighbone away from the flesh, using the tip of your knife to scrape or cut away the meat holding the bone in place, then repeat for the drumstick, plucking the bone away from the meat. Repeat for the other leg. Add the bones to the bowl.

Remove the wing bones: from inside the chicken, make a few cuts around the joint until you can press the flesh away from the bone and pull it out. Repeat for the other wing. Add the bones to the bowl.

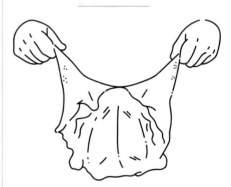

The goal is to completely bone out a whole chicken with all of the skin intact, save for the one cut you'll make down the backbone.

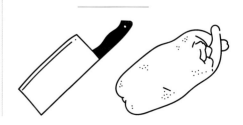

STUFF/ROLL/COOK THE CHICKEN

Clean and dry your cutting board, then lay a few long pieces of plastic wrap on top to cover it—you should have about 6 inches on each side of the chicken. Lay the chicken skin-side down in the middle of the plastic. Place the fillets in any spaces that are without meat—the idea is to have one layer of skin and one layer of meat, so trim and fill where necessary.

Season the meat generously with salt and freshly ground black pepper. Spread the Chicken Stuffing evenly across the chicken, leaving about an inch on each side of the rectangle for rolling. Nestle the ham batons on top of the stuffing about an inch or so apart. Place the prunes along each slice of ham and sprinkle with pistachios.

> The key is not packing it too tightly or over-seasoning the stuff in the middle. You want it to taste like chicken. You don't want something smooth that looks like you've meat-glued the thing together.

Starting from the side nearest you, pull the plastic wrap up and begin rolling the chicken onto itself to form a tight log. Use as much plastic wrap as you need to secure the roll. Once the roll is uniform and tight, twist the ends. With kitchen twine, tie off one end. Even out the roll (if any was pushed in from the twist) and tie off, then secure at least eight ties around the rest of the roll. Trim any excess twine.

> Plastic wrap is your friend—it helps keep it all together, like a big chicken sushi mat. Any holes in this end up getting fixed when you roll it.

In a steam oven or bamboo steamer, steam the galantine for 1 hour and 45 minutes. Remove the galantine from the steamer and cool to room temperature. Chill in the refrigerator at least overnight before serving, though 1–2 days will further deepen the flavor.

PARTY TIME

When you're ready to serve the bird, whip up a fancy little garnish that'll make it even prettier on the plate—and make sure it's got some acid to it, because that's gonna bring that cold, fatty, perfectly stuffed chicken to life. (Daniel likes to whisk together 2 tablespoons of red wine vinegar and 6 tablespoons of olive oil, season it with salt and pepper, and toss in ½ cup of roughly chopped pistachio nutmeat.) Slice the galantine into 8–10 even rounds. Plate each round and drizzle with 1–2 spoonfuls of the dressed chopped pistachios. Sprinkle with sea salt. Voilà! **LP**

FRIED & CHICKEN FIGHT
Henry'S
24h OPEN
CAN I HAVE A SPECIAL MENU PLEASE?
SO YOU WANT THE SPECIAL HUH?
HENRY
FOLLOW ME, YOU'RE RIGHT ON TIME!
WHAT?
THE FIGHT JUST STARTED KID!
WHO YOU GONNA BET ON?
ON... ON THE DARK ONE I GUESS?
NICE! 500 BUCKS ON SPICY!
YEAH!
YOU WON KID!
G... GREAT!
SEE YOU NEXT FRIDAY MY FRIEND!
OK, SURE
HOW WAS THE NEW FRIED CHICKEN PLACE?
NEXT TIME I'LL ORDER A PIZZA.

ANDREA CHRONOPOULOS

Photographs by Gabriele Stabile   *Styled by Hannah Clark*

Chicken Tonight

Chicken: we all cook it.

Except for the vegans and stuff. (Sorry about how chickeny this issue is, vegans.) But sometimes we go to the store and stare at all the birds and bird pieces and think, "Man, I don't know what to cook for dinner tonight."

So here's a roundup of recipes broken down the way chickens are broken down in the store. We've got the parts and whole birds. Nothing wild. Solid, simple, home-cookin' chicken classics to help get dinner on the table.

By Mary-Frances Heck

Roast Chicken

Roasting a whole chicken in a hot oven is one of the few reliable pleasures in life. Here's our favorite basic formula; the seasoning is endlessly variable.

MAKES 2 TO 4 SERVINGS

1 3–4 lb chicken
1 t kosher salt
2 T butter or olive oil
+ peeled and quartered onions, garlic cloves, and/or carrots
+ fresh herbs and/or sliced lemons

1. At least 12 hours in advance, sprinkle your chicken all over with the salt. Leave in the refrigerator uncovered; this lets the meat absorb the salt and the skin dry out.

2. When you're ready to cook, heat the oven to 400°F.

3. Rub the chicken with the butter or olive oil and set it in a roasting pan fitted with a roasting rack or on top of a bed of the onions, garlic, and/or carrots. Place enough herbs and lemons in the cavity to fill it. Roast the chicken for 60–65 minutes, until the skin is rendered, crispy, and browned and the middle of the breast and the joint where the thigh meets the body registers 160°F on a thermometer. Remove from the oven and let rest 10 minutes before carving.

HOW TO CARVE A CHICKEN

Lift the chicken from the roasting pan and tilt the cavity toward the pan, draining any juices into it. Place the chicken on a cutting board. With a sharp knife, slit the skin where the thighs meet the breasts. Underneath, pools of clearish juice will have collected under the skin, between the muscles.

Gently press the legs away from the body, then pick up one leg, with your thumbs near the opening and your fingers under the thigh. Press up with your fingers, cracking the "hip" joint. Slice to free the joint and set the leg aside. Repeat with the remaining leg.

Flip the legs skin-side down on the cutting board and slice through the line of fat that divides the leg and thigh. (This line of fat indicates the knee joint below. A little practice will help in making this a clean cut.) Set the thighs and drumsticks on a platter.

With the tip of your knife, draw a circle around the joint where the wing meets the body of the chicken. Twist the wing to break the joint, then use the knife to cut through any connecting cartilage. Repeat with the other wing. If desired, cut through the wing joints to yield drumettes, flats, and tips.

Insert the tip of the knife into the left breast, just left of the breastbone. Use the tip of the knife to scrape along the ribs, away from the breastbone, freeing one side of breast meat in one large piece. Trim any fat or cartilage away from the meat and skin. Set the breast aside and repeat with the remaining breast. If serving family style, slice the breasts and skin into 1-inch-thick slices and arrange on a platter with thighs, drumsticks, and wings.

Basic Poached Chicken

Poaching a whole chicken is easy and rewards laziness. The result, a pile of moist meat and a pot of rich broth, has endless uses.

MAKES 2 TO 4 SERVINGS

1 3–4 lb chicken, butchered into wings, legs, backbone, and bone-in breasts
1 T kosher salt
2 carrots, peeled and sliced into 2" chunks
2 celery ribs, sliced into 2" chunks
1 large onion, peeled and sliced into 2" chunks
+ Aromatics

AROMATICS

French-ish: 1 t black peppercorns + 10 thyme sprigs + 2 bay leaves
Chinese-ish: 1" piece ginger, smashed + 4 garlic cloves + 3 scallions + 1 t white peppercorns
Mexican-ish: ½ bunch cilantro + 1 jalapeño, split lengthwise + 1 t coriander seeds

1. Combine all of the ingredients in a large pot with 8 cups of water. Set over medium heat and bring to a simmer. Cover the pot, reduce the heat to low, and simmer gently for 10 minutes.

2. Turn off the heat and let stand until breast is cooked through and broth is flavorful, about 1 hour. Remove the breast and legs to a plate (or shock in ice water if using later) and strain the broth. Remove the meat from the bones and discard the bones, then slice or shred the meat, depending on its intended use. Use the broth for clear soups or cooking rice, or reduce by half to concentrate the flavor for gravy. Broth can be frozen at any stage for up to 3 months.

French-ish: Shred meat + serve with mustard + cornichons + crusty bread (while thinking about how this is better than chicken salad.) Thicken broth with roux + simmer with diced chicken + seasonal vegetables. Serve over noodles or seal with pastry for potpie.

Chinese-ish: Cook 1 part jasmine rice in 2 parts broth + slice chicken breasts and shred leg quarters + serve with cups of hot broth + soy-ginger dipping sauce + sliced cucumbers + cilantro.

Mexican-ish: Shred chicken + purée 1 cup chopped onion + ¼ cup tomato paste + 3 garlic cloves + 1 T ancho chili powder until smooth. Heat 1 T neutral oil in a stock pot over medium heat and add the purée. Cook, folding with a spatula, until very thick, about 8 minutes. Add the broth and 1 t dried epazote or oregano and simmer until flavors meld, about 15 minutes. Stir in shredded chicken + serve with tortilla chips + avocado + *crema* + shredded cheese.

Chicken Piccata

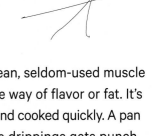

Chicken breast is a lean, seldom-used muscle that offers little in the way of flavor or fat. It's best pounded thinly and cooked quickly. A pan sauce made from the drippings gets punch from lemon and capers, and gives a reason for putting the often-underwhelming meat on the dinner table.

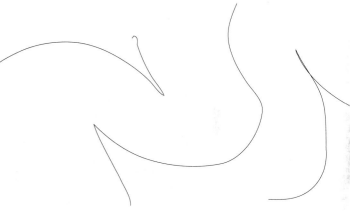

MAKES 1 TO 2 SERVINGS

1 large boneless, skinless chicken breast, about 12 oz

+ kosher salt

+ freshly ground black pepper

½ C all-purpose flour

2 T neutral oil

¼ C unsalted butter

1 shallot, finely chopped

¼ C white wine

¼ C lemon juice

½ C chicken stock

2 T capers, rinsed or drained

2 T finely chopped parsley

1. Butterfly the breast: Lay the chicken breast on a work surface with the pointed end closest to you. Stabilize it with one hand and, beginning at the fat end of the breast, use a thin, sharp knife to make a parallel cut in the side. Slice until you're within ½ inch of the seam of the breast, then open it like a book.

2. Lay the butterflied breast between two sheets of plastic wrap and use a meat mallet or small saucepan to pound it flat. Don't pound it like a hammer—starting from the center, whack the chicken with a down-and-outward motion, like tracing petals on a daisy. Continue whacking in this fashion until the meat has grown to twice its initial area and is no more than ½ inch thick.

3. Season the chicken lightly with salt and pepper. Put the flour on a plate and dredge the chicken, shaking off excess flour so there is a light, dry coating all over the chicken.

4. Heat the oil and 2 tablespoons of the butter in a 12-inch skillet over medium-high heat. Lay the chicken into the pan and cook, swirling the pan occasionally to ensure the chicken is not sticking, until browned, about 3 minutes. Flip the chicken and continue cooking until browned and nearly cooked through, about 3 minutes longer. Remove the chicken and set on a plate.

5. Add the shallot to the pan and cook until soft, about 2 minutes. Deglaze the pan with the wine, scraping up the browned bits at the bottom of the pan. When it begins to bubble, add the lemon juice and broth. Bring to a boil and cook until reduced by half, about 6 minutes. Stir in the remaining butter, capers, and parsley, then return the chicken to the pan. Simmer for 1 minute, then transfer the chicken to a large plate. Pour the sauce over the chicken and serve.

Grilled or Roasted Bone-In Chicken Breasts

Taking the time to brine and properly cook a bone-in breast will get you juicy, flavorful chicken that dark-meat folks almost won't complain about. Drying the chicken out, uncovered, for a few hours (or up to a day) in the refrigerator ahead of roasting will help yield the crispiest skin.

MAKES 2 TO 4 SERVINGS

2 bone-in, skin-on chicken breasts, about 3 lbs
+ Chicken Brine
¼ C *herbes de Provence*
2 T olive oil

1. Submerge the chicken in the Chicken Brine and place in the refrigerator. Brine the chicken for at least 4 hours and no more than 24 hours. Remove from the brine and pat dry.

2. Combine the herbes de Provence and olive oil in a small bowl. Rub the mixture all over the chicken, making sure to coat it in the herbs. Set the chicken skin-side up on a rack set inside a rimmed baking sheet or roasting pan. Hold the chicken in the refrigerator, uncovered, for at least 2 hours and preferably 24 hours.

3. If roasting: Heat the oven to 375°F. Transfer the pan with the chicken to the middle rack of the oven and roast until the center of the breasts is 155°F, about 50–55 minutes.

4. If grilling: Build a medium fire in a charcoal grill and arrange the coals for two-zone grilling (i.e., bank the coals against one side of the grill, so there's a hot part and a less hot part).

Cook the breasts over the coals, turning often, until the skin is crisp, about 10 minutes. Arrange the breasts over indirect heat with the bone side on the grill grates. Cover the grill and cook for an additional 30–40 minutes, until the chicken is cooked through.

5. Let chicken breasts rest for 10 minutes before carving from the bone and slicing.

Chicken Brine

MAKES 8 CUPS

8 C water
½ C kosher salt
¼ C sugar
1½ t black peppercorns
1 small white onion, thinly sliced
6 garlic cloves, smashed
2 bay leaves

Stir the ingredients in a large container until the salt and sugar are dissolved.

Cornell Chicken

This dish comes from the same place as chicken nuggets—Ithaca, New York, home to Cornell University. Cornell chicken combines many ingredients a university agricultural program in upstate New York would want to put to use: chicken, eggs, cider, and herbs. But its popularity isn't a by-product of its backstory; the technique is unique and its results are compelling. The marinade is super acidic, which breaks down and tenderizes the meat (don't let it soak for more than four hours, as the meat will begin to pickle and the cooked chicken will be dry); the egg helps the marinade thicken and crisp as the chicken cooks. Serve it with Syracuse salt potatoes for the full upstate effect.

MAKES 6 SERVINGS

1 egg
¾ C vegetable oil
¾ C apple-cider vinegar
2 T poultry seasoning
1 ½ T kosher salt
1 t freshly ground black pepper
6 chicken legs, about 3 lbs
+ neutral oil, for grill grates

1. Blend the egg, oil, vinegar, poultry seasoning, salt, and pepper until smooth and creamy. Place the chicken legs in a baking dish or gallon-sized ziplock bag and pour the marinade over the chicken. Seal the bag and knead the marinade around, coating the chicken evenly. Cover in the refrigerator for 2–4 hours.

2. Build a medium fire in a charcoal grill and arrange the coals for two-zone grilling (i.e., bank the coals against one side of the grill, so there's a hot part and a less hot part) or heat the oven to 500°F and turn on the broiler. Remove the chicken from the marinade, allowing the excess to drip off. Sear the chicken over medium heat on the grill or under the broiler, turning often and basting with the marinade, for 10–15 minutes, until the skin is crisped and golden. Move the chicken to indirect heat on the grill or into a 500°F oven and continue cooking, turning every 8–10 minutes and basting with the marinade, until cooked through, about 25 minutes longer. Let rest 5 minutes before serving.

Chicken Cacciatore

As with all braises, this one tastes best the next day.

MAKES 4 TO 6 SERVINGS

3 lbs chicken legs, about 6
+ kosher salt
+ freshly ground black pepper
1 T olive oil
4 garlic cloves, chopped
2 red bell peppers, cut into 1" strips
1 large yellow onion, roughly chopped
3 C button or cremini mushrooms, sliced
1 T chopped rosemary
1 t dried oregano
1 t red pepper flakes
1 C white wine
1 T red wine vinegar
1 28-oz can whole peeled tomatoes, crushed by hand
½ C pitted, brined olives
2 T chopped fresh parsley

1. Season the chicken with salt and pepper. Heat the oil in a large Dutch oven over medium-high heat. Working in batches, add the chicken, skin-side down, and sear until browned, 5–6 minutes. Flip and sear the bone side until browned, about 3–4 minutes. Transfer the chicken to a plate.

2. Heat the oven to 350°F.

3. Add the garlic, peppers, and onion to the pot and sweat the vegetables until the onions are translucent around the edges, about 5 minutes. Add the mushrooms and continue cooking until the vegetables are soft and their juices have evaporated, about 5 minutes. Stir in the rosemary, oregano, and red pepper flakes, then add the wine and vinegar, scrape the bottom of the pot, and cook until almost evaporated, about 4 minutes. Add the tomatoes and bring the sauce up to a simmer. Return the chicken to the pan and scatter the olives over the top.

4. Slide the pan into the oven. Braise the chicken until tender and the sauce has thickened, about 1 hour. Let rest at least 30 minutes. Scatter with the parsley before serving.

Pan-Roasted Chicken Thighs

This recipe allows chicken thighs, the most flavorful and texturally pleasing cut of chicken, to shine in all their unadulterated glory. Serve simply with a lemon wedge or hot sauce.

MAKES 2 SERVINGS

4 bone-in, skin-on chicken thighs, about 1½ lbs
+ kosher salt

1. Heat the oven to 375°F. Pat the chicken skin dry with a paper towel. Season the chicken thighs with salt and arrange them skin-side down in a cold 12-inch cast-iron skillet. If no cast-iron skillet exists in your life, brush an oven-safe stainless-steel skillet with 1 teaspoon of neutral oil before adding the chicken.

2. Set the skillet over medium-low heat, allowing the chicken skin to warm slowly and render its subcutaneous fat. Warm the chicken in this manner until a pool of fat forms in the pan and the skin is crisp, around 12–15 minutes, adjusting the heat as needed to maintain a persistent sizzle. Once the skin is golden and crisp, pour off all but 1 tablespoon of the fat and flip the chicken.

3. Place the skillet in the oven and roast it until the thighs are cooked through and an instant-read thermometer inserted at the bone reads 160°F, about 15–20 minutes. Transfer to a platter to rest.

Tandoori-Style Chicken

Scoring meat and marinating it in spiced yogurt helps tenderize flavorful boneless, skinless chicken thighs, a cut perfectly suited to strong spices like garam masala, paprika, turmeric, and cayenne, which give tandoori chicken its iconic reddish hue. We like it with basmati rice and *raita*, or made into a sandwich with a flatbread like naan (or pita, if we're all being honest here).

MAKES 4 TO 6 SERVINGS

3 lbs boneless, skinless chicken thighs
1 C whole-milk yogurt
¼ C neutral oil
2 T lime juice
1 4" piece peeled ginger, sliced
12 garlic cloves
2 T ground coriander
2 T garam masala
2 T sweet paprika
2 T kosher salt
2 t cumin seeds
1 T ground turmeric
1 T ground cayenne
+ Tandoori Rub

TANDOORI RUB
1 T ground fenugreek
1 t freshly ground black pepper
1 t ground cumin
1 t ground coriander
¼ t garlic powder
¼ t onion powder

1. Arrange the chicken on a cutting board. Using a small, sharp knife, diagonally score the chicken ¼-inch deep at 1-inch intervals, with 3–4 slashes per thigh. This will help the marinade penetrate the chicken and allow the chicken to cook faster.

2. Combine the yogurt, oil, lime juice, ginger, garlic, and spices in a blender and process until smooth.

3. Place the chicken in a gallon-sized ziplock bag and pour the marinade over the chicken. Seal the bag and knead the marinade around, coating the chicken evenly. Marinate the chicken for at least 4 hours and up to 12 hours.

4. Meanwhile, combine the ingredients for the Tandoori Rub in a small bowl.

5. Heat a grill to medium-high or an oven to 500°F. Remove the chicken from the marinade and scrape off any excess. Sprinkle the Tandoori Rub on both sides of the thighs, then grill, covered, or roast, turning often, until cooked through, 20–25 minutes. Uncover the grill and move the chicken to direct heat or put it under the broiler. Cook, turning once, until lightly charred, about 6 minutes. Let rest for 10 minutes and serve.

Drumsticks in Fish-Sauce Caramel

Drumsticks reward intentional, bold seasoning and attentive cooking. This Vietnamese-inspired braise-n-glaze is just that sort of thing.

MAKES 4 TO 6 SERVINGS

3 lbs drumsticks (10–14 pieces)
½ C sugar
¼ C hot water
2 C chicken broth
½ C fish sauce
2 T soy sauce

2 T *sambal oelek* or *sriracha*, optional
1 t kosher or sea salt
½ t freshly ground white pepper
3 shallots, halved
1 2" piece ginger
1 head garlic, halved crosswise
½ bunch cilantro, leaves and
   stems separated, stems tied in a bundle
   with kitchen twine
2 T lime juice

1. Arrange the drumsticks in a single layer in a large Dutch oven or large, deep skillet.

2. Heat the sugar in a small skillet over high heat and cook, swirling occasionally, until the sugar turns a dark, brick-red-colored caramel, about 3 minutes. Remove the skillet from the heat and immediately pour in the hot water. Return the skillet to medium heat and stir until the caramel dissolves. Pour the caramel sauce into a large bowl, then stir in the broth, fish sauce, soy sauce, sambal oelek, salt, white pepper, shallots, ginger, garlic, and cilantro stems. Pour the liquid and aromatics over the chicken, toss to coat, and refrigerate for at least 4 hours or overnight.

3. Transfer the pot to the stove and bring to a simmer over high heat. Reduce the heat to maintain a steady simmer, cover the pot, and cook the chicken for 20 minutes. Uncover the pot and continue cooking, turning the chicken every few minutes, until the chicken is cooked through and the sauce is reduced and thick and coating the drumsticks, about 15 minutes more. Remove the pan from the heat, stir in the lime juice, and let the chicken rest for 15 minutes in the liquid.

4. Scatter the chicken with the cilantro leaves and serve.

Jerk Chicken

The key flavors in jerk are thyme, all-spice, and Scotch bonnet peppers. It likes when you add the smoky char of a grill to that mix, but even in the oven it comes out right. Best served with lime wedges and a cold Red Stripe.

MAKES 4 TO 6 SERVINGS

3 lbs drumsticks (10–12 pieces)
8 garlic cloves
2 Scotch bonnet peppers, stems removed
1 2" piece ginger, peeled and sliced
¾ C chopped scallions (about 4)
¼ C thyme leaves
⅓ C lime juice
⅓ C olive oil
2 T honey
1 T allspice berries
1 T kosher or sea salt

1. Arrange the drumsticks on a cutting board and use a small, sharp knife to diagonally score the chicken down to the bone at 1-inch intervals, 3–4 slashes per drumstick. This will help the marinade penetrate the chicken and allow the chicken to cook faster.

2. Combine the garlic, peppers, ginger, scallions, thyme, lime juice, oil, honey, allspice, and salt in a blender and process until smooth.

3. Place the drumsticks in a gallon-sized ziplock bag and pour the marinade over the chicken. Seal the bag and knead the marinade around, coating the chicken evenly. Marinate the chicken for at least 12 hours and up to 2 days.

4. Heat a grill to medium high or an oven to 500°. Remove the chicken from the marinade and scrape off any excess. Grill, covered, or roast the chicken, turning often, until charred and cooked through, 25–30 minutes.

Orange-Sesame Chicken Wings

Braising chicken wings yields tender, silky meat and skin. Covering them in an orange-sesame glaze yields nostalgic feelings about take-out Chinese food.

MAKES 4 SERVINGS

⅓ **C + 1 T** fresh orange juice

1 T orange zest

2 T soy sauce

2 T light brown sugar

1 T rice vinegar

1 t chopped or grated fresh ginger

1 t chopped or grated garlic

¼ **t** toasted sesame oil

¼ **t** red pepper flakes

¼ **C** water

2 lbs chicken wings, separated into flats and drumettes

+ kosher salt

1 T neutral oil

1 t cornstarch

1 T toasted sesame seeds

+ steamed white rice, for serving (optional)

1. In a small bowl, whisk together the ⅓ cup orange juice, orange zest, soy sauce, brown sugar, vinegar, ginger, garlic, sesame oil, red pepper flakes, and water, until the sugar is dissolved.

2. Season the chicken wings with a little salt. Heat the oil in a large skillet or wok over medium-high heat. Working in 2 batches, add the chicken wings and cook, turning frequently in the pan, until they are golden brown, about 4 minutes. Add half the sauce and bring to a simmer. Reduce heat to medium and gently simmer, until the chicken wings are cooked through and the sauce has reduced by a third, 10–12 minutes.

3. Stir the cornstarch with the remaining tablespoon of orange juice in a bowl, then stir half the mixture into the sauce and return to a full boil, folding the wings in the sauce until they are coated. Repeat with second batch. Combine the two batches of chicken, sprinkle with sesame seeds, and toss once again. Serve with steamed white rice.

Tsukune (Japanese Meatballs)

In general, ground chicken is the sketchiest meat at the market, and chicken meatballs are notoriously dry and spongy. But *yakitori*—the charcoal-fueled Japanese style of grilling where every part of the bird is celebrated and elevated—points the direction toward meatball irresistibility. The trick is cooking a portion—say a quarter by weight—of the ground chicken meat before mixing the meatballs. This step gives textural variation within the meatball and provides an insurance policy against toughness.

MAKES 4 SERVINGS

1 lb ground chicken thighs
1 C finely chopped scallions (about 6)
1½ t kosher salt
+ vegetable oil
+ Tare

Get freshly ground chicken for this dish: thighs are the most delicious part of the chicken, so grind boneless, skinless ones yourself (or ask your butcher to do it). If neither of these options work for you, dice your thighs, chill them in the freezer for 30 minutes, then pulse them in the food processor until very finely chopped.

1. Heat a small, nonstick skillet over medium heat and add a quarter of the ground chicken thighs. Cook until opaque and cooked through, chopping with a spatula as it cooks, about 3 minutes. Let cool.

2. In a medium bowl, combine the cooked and raw chicken, scallions, and salt. Mix with your hands until the meat is tacky and holds together like a kneaded dough. Alternatively, pulse in the food processor until it comes together in a ball.

3. Wash your hands, then rub them with a teaspoon of oil. Divide the meat into 12 equal balls, rolling between your hands to smooth. Thread the meatballs onto 4 skewers, leaving ¼ inch between each meatball. Arrange the meatballs on a rimmed baking sheet lined with foil.

4. Arrange a rack 2–3 inches from the broiler and heat the broiler to high. Broil the meatballs for 2 minutes, then brush them with some Tare. Return the pan to the broiler and cook, turning the meatballs and basting them every 2 minutes, until lightly charred and cooked through, 8–10 minutes longer. Let rest for a few minutes before serving.

Tare

Tare, or basting sauce, helps keep tsukune juicy and flavorful as they grill, but it's not a bad idea to make some extra for dipping later.

MAKES ½ CUP

⅓ C chicken broth
2 ½ T soy sauce
2 ½ T mirin
2 ½ T demerara sugar or rock candy
½ t black pepper
1½ t rice or sherry vinegar

Combine the broth, soy sauce, mirin, sugar, and pepper in a small saucepan and bring to a boil over medium-high heat. Reduce the heat and simmer until reduced by half, about 15 minutes. Stir in the vinegar and let cool. **LP**

Contri

Kee Byung-keun is a writer and photographer living in Tokyo. He likes to wander supermarkets to relax.

Maria Chimishkyan is an illustrator, animator, and designer based in Brooklyn. Cocreator of the notorious NYC ramen Google Doc; DM for an invite.

Andrea Chronopoulos was born in Athens in 1990 and is currently working as a freelance illustrator for magazines and children's books in Rome. She is a founding member of Studio Pilar, a creative studio based in Rome.

Ian Cumming has been a photographer for over twenty years, and in that time he has traveled the world. Closer to home, he is the Dalai Lama's photographer in the UK. He was also a finalist in the 2015 *Great British Bake Off*, so he bakes lovely bread and cakes.

Tove K. Danovich is a former New Yorker now based in Portland, Oregon. Someday, she hopes to have three chickens named Dolly, Loretta, and Patsy.

Cristina Daura, born and raised in Barcelona. She studies illustration at La Escola Massana and the Maryland Institute College of Art, in Baltimore. After working for several years as a babysitter while trying to survive in the illustration world, she now tries to survive on her work without the babysitting.

Pete Deevakul was crowned Mr. WHS, the all-male beauty pageant of Whitney High School, despite his current unshaven and, quite frankly, sloppy appearance. During this time, he dated the class president, who drove them to prom in her father's Mazda Miata. Previously, he earned a one-day suspension for an incident involving a potato projectile device.

Fuchsia Dunlop is a James Beard Award–winning writer and a cook specializing in Chinese food. She is based in London.

Gillian Ferguson is a writer and radio producer based in Los Angeles.

Matt Furie occasionally rebuilds himself out of matter grown in a state of suffering.

Pete Gamlen is an illustrator from Brexit Britain who lives in Trump's America. He eagerly awaits Satan's Hell.

Laura Goodman is a writer who lives in East London. Talk to her: @laurajgood.

Walter Green is a writer and designer based in New York. He recently vowed to never eat another chicken nugget, but we'll see how that goes.

Mary-Frances Heck is an author and food editor. Her recipes and writing have appeared in numerous cookbooks and magazines, including *Lucky Peach, Bon Appétit, Saveur, Cooking Light, Redbook, Rodale's Organic Life, Fitness,* and *Rachael Ray Every Day.* Her first cookbook, *Sweet Potatoes,* will be published by Clarkson Potter in September 2017.

Johnathon Kelso is an Atlanta-based photographer documenting life in the South. To view more of his work, please visit johnathonkelso.com.

E. Jeffrey Kriksciun seeks the strange out of the mundane. His favorite breakfast item is a smoothie stuffed with as many mangoes and greens as possible.

Tim Lahan is an artist, illustrator, and the author of *The Nosyhood,* a kids' book from

butors

McSweeney's. He's seen a chicken fly, but he's not ruling out that it actually may have been a pigeon, now that he thinks about it.

Sarah Lammer is an artist and illustrator into making images, public drawing, collaborative projects, and open-faced sandwiches.

John Lisle was born a preemie on Halloween in Canada, and is currently working as a freelance illustrator and art director in Brooklyn.

Molly Matalon is a twenty-five-year-old photographer with a BFA in photography from the School of Visual Arts. She currently lives in the Bay Area working as a photographer for hire and making personal work at the same time.

David Matthews is a writer and former chef based in Sydney. He's the senior sub-editor and features writer for *delicious.* magazine, holds a master's in food studies, and has presented on topics such as *terroir* and food criticism at food symposia, including MAD. He also occasionally writes about sports.

Harold McGee writes about the chemistry of food and cooking. He is the author of *On Food and Cooking*, *The Curious Cook*, and *Keys to Good Cooking*.

Jim Meehan, a bar operator, educator, and author of *The PDT Cocktail Book*, worked at some of New York City's most popular restaurants and bars, including Gramercy Tavern and the Pegu Club, before opening the James Beard Award–winning bar PDT in 2007. The former editor of *Food & Wine magazine*'s annual cocktail book and the *Mr. Boston: Official Bartender's Guide*, Meehan currently serves as the drinks editor for Tasting Table, the global ambassador for Banks Rum, and the curator of the cocktail programs for American Express Centurion lounges nationally.

Tamara Micner is a journalist, playwright, and recent vegan who calls London home. She hails from Vancouver and cooks with her roommate just about every day. tamaramicner.com.

Chris Nuttall-Smith is a food writer and restaurant critic based in Toronto.

Pete Sharp grew up in the Midlands and studied illustration at the University of Brighton before moving to South London, where he worked for two years in printmaking and now works out of a railway-arch studio as a full-time freelance artist. He's particularly interested in the use of color being informed by the limitations of the print process and likes to keep his work style as varied as possible as he draws inspiration from so many different areas of art and design.

Richt has been painting since 2002 and is an established graffiti artist and illustrator. He has exhibited his work across the UK and Europe, with solo shows in Barcelona, Amsterdam, London, and his native Bristol. His work has been featured in magazines and publications across the globe for graffiti and street art, including the highly influential Street Sketchbook by Tristan Manco (Thames and Hudson, 2007). Find him on Instagram: @richtpaint.

Kelsey Wroten is an illustrator and cartoonist who hails from Kansas City, Missouri. Her favorite things are cats, coffee, and Buffy the Vampire Slayer.